THE

"I Could Eat

PASTA

Every Night"

COOKBOOK

Also by Susan Kosoff

GOOD OLD-FASHIONED CAKES

GOOD OLD-FASHIONED COOKIES

COOKING WITH FIVE INGREDIENTS OR LESS

THE

"I Could Eat
PASTA
Every Night"
COOKBOOK

Susan Kosoff

Illustrations by
Steven Salerno

ST. MARTIN'S GRIFFIN ❧ NEW YORK

Display typeface set in Random House and Birdhouse
Designed by SONGHEE KIM

Library of Congress Cataloging-in-Publication Data

Kosoff, Susan.
      The "I could eat pasta every night" cookbook / by Susan Kosoff. —
1st St. Martin's Griffin ed.
        p. cm.
      ISBN 0-312-14359-1
      1. Cookery (Pasta)   2. Cookery, Italian.   3. Quick and easy cookery.
4. Low-fat diet—Recipes.   I. Title.
TX809.M17K657 1996
641.8'22—dc20   96-5171
                                                     CIP

First St. Martin's Griffin Edition: July 1995

10 9 8 7 6 5 4 3 2

For DAVID, SHEILA, GINNY, JEFF,

MELISSA, JOE, CAROL, AND JON;

and for my sister, LYDIA SCHWARZ

Thank you, thank you, thank you

ABOVE ALL, TO MY FAMILY—PAUL, MARK, AND JORDAN
(WHO SURVIVED YET ANOTHER BOOK!)
FOR THEIR ETERNAL LOVE, GOOD SPIRITS, AND WONDERFUL
SENSE OF HUMOR.

and

TO MY CHERISHED FRIEND DEBORAH MINTCHEFF FOR
UNSELFISHLY SHARING HER INFINITE WISDOM, CREATIVE TALENT,
AND IMPECCABLE GOOD TASTE.

and

TO MY EDITOR BARBARA ANDERSON, FOR HER SUPPORT AND
INVALUABLE ADVICE, AND TO JOY CHANG FOR HER ENTHUSIASM
AND EXPERT EDITING.

and

TO MINI SHADE AND DENNIS DUGAN, FOR SHARING THEIR HOME
COMPUTER AT THE ELEVENTH HOUR!

CONTENTS

In Praise of PASTA

Pasta is the perfect panacea for hunger in my home. Its great taste, nutritional value, and easy prep time provide a quick cure for feeding a family that is constantly on the run—without putting a hole in my pocket. Regardless of whether you're cooking for one or twenty, serving pasta as often as possible probably makes sense for you, too. Considering that pasta tastes good with almost everything, the permutations are endless. If the many different sizes and shapes of pasta spin your head around, look on the bright side: With so many choices, you can create a different pasta every day without duplicating the same dish. When we're really in a hurry, we enjoy toppings that cook in the same amount of time as it takes to boil the pasta. Without hesitation, pasta is the food we sit down to and fill up on most often.

You can purchase inexpensive, domestic dried pasta, which is readily available and tastes very good—or you can spend slightly more on imported Italian dried pasta. Imported pastas have popped up in almost every area these days—and with good reason. They taste superior to domestic brands, stay "al dente" longer, and are generally worth the price. They may be harder to locate in some regions, but if you stumble on a box of imported pasta, treat yourself. My own personal favorites are DeCecco and Barilla, but you should try other brands and decide for yourself.

Pasta packs nutritional value into your diet. It's not only a good source of complex carbohydrates and minerals, but also contains six of the eight essential amino acids—which means you're getting protein as well. When prepared without smothering sauces, the fat and calorie content in pasta is naturally low.

Pasta is a nourishing alternative to meat. Current nutritional studies indicate that eating more carbohydrates, significantly less fat, and moderate amounts of protein reduces calorie consumption. Studies also suggest that a diet high in complex carbohydrates is healthier than one that highlights meat and dairy products. The USDA Food Guide Pyramid bears out the health benefits of consuming foods low in fat and high in complex carbohydrates. The composition of the pyramid's broad base contains a balance of grains, vegetables, and fruits, with a considerably smaller portion at the top earmarked for eggs, dairy, meat, fish, and fats.

Switching to a healthier diet may change your ideas of what constitutes a meal. The typical model of a main meal complemented by side dishes no longer seems ideal. When planning a menu, think more about eating meals made up of compatible foods. The answer to the question "What's for dinner?" might be unpredictable, including many different foods that together provide a balanced and healthy meal. You can serve two different, but complementary, pasta dishes, for instance, and still be eating smart. Promote your health and the health of your family by including a crisp green salad, steamed vegetables, or other healthy foods, too.

Last but not least, please savor the taste of pasta and other foods. People who profess that food is unimportant amaze me, and I think miss out on a pleasurable experience. As far as I can tell, taste is every bit as important as the other four senses. All are functional, but each one brings joy as well.

Throughout these pages you'll find helpful hints, shopping tips, and fun facts about pasta and other ingredients. The recipes are easy to follow and kitchen friendly—the majority of them cook in one skillet on top of the stove.

So pull out the pot, gather the ingredients you need, and cook a simple pasta dish tonight. After that, just sit back and accept the applause.

PASTA

Shapes

THE LONG AND SHORT OF IT

Choosing the perfect pasta for a particular sauce can be confusing and time-consuming. Well, ponder no more. Forget about any real and hard fast rules when it comes to selecting pasta. Instead, use your own "noodle" and decide what pastas you like best based on what's available in your area, and more important, what you have in your pantry. Treat the following list as a general guide to selecting which sauce "sits" best on the various pasta shapes: smooth-surfaced, thick tubular shapes (penne, ziti, or mezzani) generally go best with thick sauces that cling to their surfaces; ridged, grooved, or spiral-shaped pastas (fusilli, rotelle, or any of the rigati family) are perfect for holding a less-thick sauce; spaghetti and ribbon-shaped pastas are best served with more delicate sauces. As you experiment, you'll teach yourself how to narrow the number of varieties to choose from (more than 100 in some regions) for any given recipe. In the end, the choice is always yours.

Cook with confidence. Familiarize yourself with all the different endings given to the names of Italian pastas, since the ending often reveals the pasta size. For instance, pasta names ending with *-ini, -ina, -iti,* or *-elle* imply that the pasta is relatively small or thin, while names ending with *-oni* suggest a larger-shaped pasta. A ridged or grooved pasta has *rigati* at the end of its name.

SPAGHETTI FAMILY

Spaghetti ("a length of cord") and all other members in this family tend to be on the thin side. They supply the best background for oil, garlic, and butter-based sauces, as well as light tomato sauces.

Angel Hair. See *capellini.*

Bucatini. This is a thick spaghetti with a narrow hole through the middle.

Capellini ("fine hairs"). Also known as *angel hair,* these thin strands of pasta are best when served with light, delicate sauces or in soups.

Fusilli ("twisted spaghetti"). This long, hollow, spiral-shaped pasta goes well with garlic and oil-based sauces. Use short fusilli in pasta salads, or with tomato-based or cheese-based sauces.

Perciatelli. Similar to *bucatini,* but fatter.

Spaghettini ("little lengths of cord"). This pasta is actually the same length as *spaghetti,* only thinner.

Vermicelli ("little worms"). These are fine strands of spaghetti that are slightly thicker than capellini. They are sold straight or occasionally in coils.

RIBBON FAMILY

Fettuccine ("small ribbons"). Widely available either fresh or dried, plain or flavored (such as spinach or tomato), this pasta shape ranges in size from 1/16 inch to 3 inches wide.

Linguine ("little tongues"). Long and thin, this flat ribbonlike pasta goes well with delicately flavored sauces.

Pappardelle. This is a lasagne-style, wavy edge, ribbon pasta about 1 1/4 inches wide. It is made with eggs and therefore has its own distinctive flavor. Chicken and meat sauces, as well as tomato and cream-based sauces, work well with this pasta.

Tagliatelle (from *tagliare*, to cut). Flat, long, and a bit wider than *fettuccine*, these ribbonlike strips were supposedly inspired by the beautiful blond tresses of a 16th-century woman. *Tagliarini* are narrow tagliatelle.

Short Pasta

Bow Ties. See *farfalle*.

Cavatelli. This is a hollow, narrow shell with a rippled surface. It's good in light soups.

Egg Noodles. These are available in different widths. Serve them alone, topped with a sauce, or prepared in soups, salads, and casseroles.

Elbow Macaroni. These short, curved tubes are available in many sizes. Use tiny elbows for soup, medium to large ones for casseroles, salads, and sauced dishes.

Farfalle ("butterflies"). Most commonly known as *bow ties*, this pasta shape tastes great with all kinds of sauces—from olive-oil-based, tomato, and light meat sauces to sauces made with small pieces of vegetables.

Gemelli ("twins"). This pasta shape looks like two short pieces of spaghetti twisted together. Serve with a chunky sauce.

Mezzani. This is a 1- to 2-inch-long tubular pasta with a smooth exterior. Use as you would penne.

Mostaccioli ("small mustaches"). These 2-inch, medium-size tubes have diagonally cut ends. Serve with a chunky sauce.

Orecchiette ("little ears"). This medium-size, disk-shaped pasta goes well with olive-oil-based sauces, tomato sauces, light meat sauces, and sauces made with small pieces of vegetables.

Penne ("quills"). These are narrow tubes about 2 inches long with ends cut diagonally like a quill pen. Use with thick meat sauces, olive-oil-based sauces, sauces with chunks of vegetables, sauces with ricotta or cottage cheese, and for baked pasta dishes.

Radiatore ("radiator"). This short, fat pasta shape is ruffled and ridged like a radiator. They are sold in a variety of flavors, including plain, and make an interesting addition to soups, salads, and entrées.

Rigatoni. These are large grooved tubes. See *penne*.

Rotelle ("small wheels"). See *route*.

Rotini. This corkscrew-shaped pasta is perfect for creamy or chunky sauces.

Route ("wagon wheels"). This pasta shape goes well with soups and salads. Use it with olive-oil and tomato-based sauces, or add chunks of meat, chicken, or vegetables.

Tortellini ("little twists"). These are filled with meat, cheese, or sometimes puréed vegetables. They are sold fresh, frozen, and dried. Use them in salads, broth, and with light sauces.

Ziti ("bridegrooms"). This tubular macaroni is either straight or slightly curved. It is most often cut into short pieces, but it can be very long, too. Ziti is most often used in baked pasta dishes and in rich meaty dishes, but I've used ziti in salads with great success.

VERY SHORT PASTAS

Alphabets. These small letters are perfect for soup or broth. Children appreciate them as an alternative to potatoes or rice when served as a side dish.

Ancini Pepe ("peppercorns"). These are tiny pieces of cut spaghetti for serving in soup or broth.

Couscous. An import from North Africa, these tiny beads of pasta cook almost instantly. Couscous is made of semolina wheat flour mixed with water, which has been pushed through a sieve to make fine grains. The texture is light and fluffy, perfect for salads and as a bed for vegetables, beef, or chicken.

Ditali ("thimbles"). Ditali is the same size and shape as a thimble, but with both ends chopped off. *Ditalini* is a smaller version of ditali and is easier to find in supermarkets. Use in soups or as a side dish with a light tomato sauce.

Orzo. This rice-shaped pasta is good in soups or as a side dish, served with an olive-oil-based, butter, or light tomato sauce.

Stellini ("little stars"). This tiny star-shaped pasta is best in broth or other light soup. Children like "stars" served with butter and a pinch of salt.

Tripolini ("little bows"). These are small, rounded *bow ties*. Use in soup or as a side dish.

What to Have on Hand

THE INGREDIENTS AND EQUIPMENT
THAT MAKE LIFE EASY

POWER IN THE PANTRY

The shelf life of good-quality, commercially dried pasta is approximately three years, so stockpiling a variety of shapes and sizes makes sense. If shelf space is limited, concealing unopened pasta in a shoe-box-sized *plastic* box may be the solution. Close the box with a tight-fitting lid and store in a convenient spot. Then, with plenty of fresh vegetables and a selection of the following basic items on hand, you're only minutes away from a quick, delicious, and healthy meal.

OLIVE OILS

Use *extra-virgin* olive oil on salads, in marinades, dressings, and when you want to dip bread into something pure and delicious. This premium oil is made from the first pressing of the olive, without using heat or chemicals in the process. The fruity aroma and flavor of this raw oil complements tomatoes, vegetables, chicken, herbs, and other additions to pasta. A small amount of this flavorful oil goes a long way—a big boost when cutting down on calories and cholesterol. *Virgin* olive oil comes from the second pressing, with a flavor that can range from lightly fruity to sweet and nutty. It, too, is excellent for all the above-mentioned uses, and is slightly less expensive. Use this oil to cook onions or garlic, or whenever the oil remains a part of the dish, as in Pesto (page 25). Pure olive oil is produced by treating the previously pressed pulp with chemical solvents. It has a faint taste of olives and is adequate for cooking. Choose a high-quality oil, whatever your needs may be. In the following recipes, "olive oil" refers to a high-quality virgin or pure olive oil.

SESAME OIL

Sesame oil can be found in most large supermarkets and specialty stores. Use this oil sparingly in dressings and marinades.

TOMATOES

Use fresh, ripe, flavorful tomatoes when they're in season. Store them at room temperature, and use as soon as possible. Very soft, ripe tomatoes spoil quickly in heat. Store those tomatoes in the refrigerator. The rest of the year stock up on good-quality domestic or imported Italian-style canned plum tomatoes. Avoid packaged tomatoes and the tasteless fresh tomatoes commonly found in supermarkets.

VINEGAR

This may seem extravagant, but having a 12-ounce bottle of each one of the following vinegars makes for more interesting and diversified meals:

RED WINE VINEGAR
BALSAMIC VINEGAR
RICE VINEGAR

GARLIC AND ONIONS

For one week's worth of cooking, you need 1 to 2 heads of garlic and 1 to 2 pounds of onions. Store them at room temperature exposed to the air.

DRIED HERBS AND SPICES

Oregano, basil, and crushed red pepper flakes perk up the simplest pasta dishes, and you'll reach for them frequently. Keep all dried herbs and spices away from light, air, heat, and moisture. To retain their pungent aroma longer, store your supply in sealed glass jars. A cool dark cabinet or the back of the refrigerator is ideal—never next to the stove. Use within one year, and be sure to sniff before you season.

CANNED BROTH

Canned chicken broth and vegetable broth are convenient to use, but like anything else, some brands are better than others.

Shop around until you're satisfied with the taste—the best broth tastes rich and flavorful, not salty.

CANNED BEANS

When you have one or two cans (16 to 19 ounces each) of chickpeas, black beans, and red kidney beans, it takes little more to prepare a filling meal. Rinse and drain canned beans before use to remove excess salt, or prepare your own dried beans (at a fraction of the cost) and eliminate the salt entirely. A can of beans (16 or 19 ounces) is equal to 2 cups of prepared beans.

MISCELLANEOUS

With the advent of bulk supermarket shopping some items listed below are available in larger sizes at a fraction of the cost. Use the weights and amounts on the list as recommendations only, and if storage space is tight.

1 BOTTLE (8 OUNCES) CLAM JUICE

1 TO 3 CANS EACH TUNA, SARDINES, AND PINK SALMON

1 JAR (3 OUNCES) NONPAREIL CAPERS

1 JAR (7 OUNCES) ROASTED RED PEPPERS

1 TUBE (4 1/2 OUNCES) IMPORTED TOMATO PASTE

1 PACKAGE (ABOUT 1 OUNCE) DRIED MUSHROOMS

1 BOTTLE (5 OUNCES) LOW-SODIUM SOY SAUCE

2 OR 3 CANS (14 1/2 OR 16 OUNCES EACH) PEELED,
   WHOLE TOMATOES

2 CANS (28 OUNCES EACH) ITALIAN-STYLE PLUM TOMATOES

1 JAR (8 OUNCES) HIGH-QUALITY PREPARED SPAGHETTI SAUCE

IN THE REFRIGERATOR OR FREEZER

PARMESAN AND/OR ROMANO CHEESE

Buy fresh cheese, please—the best you can afford. Fresh cheese imparts a lot of flavor, even in small quantities, and always tastes better than prepackaged or processed brands. Buy cheese wedges—they taste fresher and cost less than grated cheese. Wrap wedges tightly in several layers of plastic wrap and store in the refrigerator to protect the flavor and freshness of the cheese. Grate as needed.

MISCELLANEOUS

- 1 BUNCH FRESH PARSLEY
- 2 OR 3 LEMONS
- 1 POUND BUTTER
- 1 JAR (8 OUNCES) DIJON MUSTARD
- 1 JAR (16 OUNCES) BRINE-CURED BLACK OLIVES
- 1 POUND GROUND TURKEY
- 2 PACKAGES (16 OUNCES EACH) FROZEN CHEESE-
  OR MEAT-FILLED PASTA
- 1 BUNCH CILANTRO, ALSO KNOWN AS CORIANDER OR
  CHINESE PARSLEY
- 1 BUNCH SCALLIONS
- 1 BUNCH CARROTS
- 1 BUNCH FRESH BROCCOLI
- 2 OR 3 BELL PEPPERS
- SALAD GREENS
- 2 PACKAGES (9 OUNCES EACH) FROZEN ARTICHOKE HEARTS

HOW TO STORE FRESH VEGETABLES

In general, vegetables prefer cool, moist conditions. Store them in sealed plastic bags in the refrigerator, if you're not cooking them on the day of purchase. Some vegetables, such as kale, carrots, celery, parsley, and fresh cilantro, keep best when misted mildly with water before bagging. Vegetables with thicker skins, such as zucchini, eggplant, and butternut squash, are better off stored dry. Stand asparagus in an inch of water and refrigerate until ready to use.

TOOLS OF THE TRADE

Some basic but essential kitchen tools belong in every working kitchen: a large covered pot, a sharp chef's knife, a liquid measuring cup, a set of dry measuring cups, a set of measuring spoons, a timer, a vegetable peeler, and a medium-sized cutting board. These tools enable you to prepare food faster, safer, and easier. If you're just starting your culinary collection, try to obtain the following as well.

PASTA POT

Any large pot with a tight-fitting lid (a covered pot boils much more quickly than an uncovered one) is suitable as your pasta-boiling kettle. To provide ample room for the pasta to move around, the pot should hold 4 to 6 quarts of water. If you're purchasing a new pot, select one with a heavy bottom that will conduct heat evenly and prevent warping over time.

LONG-HANDLED FORK

This allows you to stir and separate the pasta as it cooks.

NONSTICK SKILLET

This skillet speaks for itself. Food won't stick to the pan's surface, which allows you to cook with less fat. A 12-inch skillet is perfect for simmering stove-top sauces and for tossing pasta and sauce together.

COLANDERS

A medium-sized and/or a large colander are the two you'll use most often. I prefer footed colanders, made from stainless steel, with handles on both sides. The stainless steel cleans quickly, the feet hold the colander above the sink floor for quicker drainage, and the handles let you shake out the water quickly.

PASTA SERVERS

There are two specialized utensils for serving pasta, and I like them both equally well. You can use stainless steel salad tongs, the kind that are hinged together at the base, or a pasta claw, available in plastic, wood, or stainless steel. Both are practical because they allow you to serve with one hand while the other hand holds the plate. Using two wooden spoons, or a wooden fork and spoon, is another way to serve the pasta.

CHEESE GRATER

Graters come in assorted shapes and sizes, but the standard flat grater or the four-sided stand-up kind is sufficient for grating small amounts of hard cheese. For larger amounts, a food processor saves time and energy.

PASTA

in the Pot

HOW TO COOK AND SERVE PERFECT PASTA

Taste pasta frequently during cooking time and always just before draining. When the pasta is slightly firm and offers some resistance when you take a bite, that's "al dente" (an Italian term that literally translates as "to the tooth"). A little practice and intuition are necessary to cook pasta until al dente, but once you know how your instincts take over. You'll be able to shift into automatic pilot and drive your taste buds crazy with great taste and texture.

COOKING PASTA

Bring 4 quarts of water to a boil in a large covered pot. Add 2 teaspoons salt, if you like. (Salt enhances the pasta's flavor, and a purist (not I) will tell you that pasta without salt is flat. I say experiment and decide for yourself. If health reasons require you to pare down your salt intake, leave it out.) Add pasta, stir, and partially cover the pot until water returns to a boil. Immediately remove cover, stir again, and cook pasta just until al dente. Reserve 1/2 cup cooking water just before draining in case you need it later. Drain remaining water from pasta and return to covered pot off the heat.

TIMING DRIED PASTA

Avoid timing dried pasta. Each pot of pasta cooks differently depending on size, thickness, and brand, and watching the clock may cause disastrous results. Pay no attention to the recommended time given on packages—it's usually too long! Instead, get into the habit of tasting the pasta periodically as it cooks. To be safe, start tasting dried commercial pasta 4 minutes after the water returns to a boil. Use tongs to pull a piece of pasta from the pot. Shake off the excess water. Wait a second or two for the pasta to cool, and then take a bite. If the pasta tastes hard, or you see a white, uncooked center, continue to cook the pasta. Test again after 1 minute passes, and several times more, if necessary, until the pasta is slightly chewy but shows no signs of an uncooked center. Drain immediately. The pasta will continue to cook as you drain and toss it with the sauce.

TIMING FRESH PASTA

Fresh pasta requires brief cooking. Always taste a piece 10 to 15 seconds after the water returns to a boil. For fresh pasta that has been frozen, cook a minute or two longer until al dente.

DRAINING PASTA

Before you drain the pasta water, ladle out about 1/2 cup cooking water and reserve for later use. Immediately drain the remaining water, using a colander large enough to hold all the pasta at once. Shake the colander to remove excess water. If the sauce requires a few minutes further cooking, return pasta to cooking pot or warm serving bowl and toss immediately with a few tablespoons reserved cooking water. Save remaining reserved water, in case you need to add more later. If you prefer, toss hot pasta with 2 to 3 teaspoons olive oil instead of water. Add sauce to hot pasta as soon as possible.

RINSING PASTA

Never rinse pasta, unless you've cooked lasagna noodles (which need to separate quickly) or pasta you plan to use in salad.

SAUCING PASTA

Recipes sometimes suggest tossing pasta and sauce together in the sauce skillet or pasta pot for a few minutes over low heat. This important step permits the pasta to absorb some of the sauce's flavor. Lift the pasta with tongs or two forks and toss to coat until the pasta heats through.

SERVING PASTA

Serve pasta on warmed serving platters and/or in warmed bowls. Avoid serving pasta in a swimming pool of sauce, since you'll only drown out its flavor and texture.

PASSING CHEESE

Use a cheese mill, a small Italian cheese grater, or the fine side of an all-purpose hand grater to grate the best-quality cheese you can afford. Instead of passing grated cheese, let everyone grate his or her own at the table.

How Much to Cook

Two to three ounces dry pasta is usually enough for each portion. As a general guide, serve the smaller portion for a first-course pasta, or when it accompanies additional dishes such as fish, meat, chicken, or another pasta dish. Use the larger portion

for main dish servings. These amounts may seem inadequate, but bear in mind that bread, salad, and possibly dessert will round out the meal. By the way, when a recipe serves four as a main dish, you can usually figure on getting six to eight first-course portions.

Most of these recipes list pasta in uncooked amounts and by weight. Use a reliable food scale, or keep portion control under check by converting the weight to cup measurements.

WEIGHED PASTA	CUP EQUIVALENT
2 ounces uncooked dry short pasta (small shapes)	1/2 cup
2 ounces uncooked dry short pasta (large shapes)	1 cup
2 ounces uncooked dry long pasta (small shapes)	3/4 inch in diameter*
3 ounces fresh long pasta	1 cup
3 ounces fresh short pasta	1 cup

PREPARING THE RECIPES

Before you try these recipes, I encourage you to read the basic cooking principles and recipe-reading hints listed below. This information will simplify and enhance your cooking experience.

1. Use only the freshest, best-quality ingredients available.

2. Take the time to "read through before you do," which means reading the entire recipe, not just the list of ingredients.

3. Gather the necessary ingredients and equipment before you start. When you know what to expect, it's easier to cook with confidence.

4. These recipes list a measured or weight quantity, such as "12 ounces penne" or "2 cups diced tomatoes" when specific amounts are necessary to the taste of the dish. When it doesn't seem to matter much, the recipe will read, for example, "1 large carrot," or "1 cup small broccoli florets." Since certain ingredients are by nature approximate, adding an inexact amount won't change the overall taste of the final dish, so use your own judgment.

5. Follow the directions carefully, but learn to rely on your own judgment too, especially with regard to cooking times.

*Hold a tight fistful of pasta 1/2 inch from its end and measure across the top.

6. Seasonings are a matter of individual taste, particularly when it comes to salt, pepper, and garlic. Again, use your own judgment.

7. Use warmed serving bowls and plates so the food stays hotter for a longer period of time. Put them in the oven several minutes before serving, and set the dial to a low temperature. After a few minutes, turn off the heat, leaving the dishes inside until needed. Serve individual portions of pasta in bowls rather than on plates whenever possible—the proximity of the pasta helps to retain the heat.

QUICK TRICKS FOR PREPARING PASTA

1. Start with very hot water from the tap and always cover the pot to speed up cooking time.

2. When you fall short of the full amount of a particular pasta for a recipe, be creative and combine similarly sized pasta to make up the difference. Just be sure to select pasta that cooks in approximately the same amount of time.

3. Drop cut-up vegetables designated for serving with the pasta into the water as pasta cooks, toward the end of pasta cooking time. Add whichever vegetables take the longest to cook first. Drain pasta and vegetables together, then quickly toss with herbs and sauce.

4. For immediate flavor, drop chopped or sliced garlic and/or selected herbs into boiling water when you add the pasta. When pasta is done, drain and toss with hot chicken or vegetable broth.

CONVERSION TABLES AND EQUIVALENTS
LIQUID VOLUME

UNITED STATES	IMPERIAL	INTERNATIONAL (METRIC)
1/2 teaspoon	1/3 tsp.	2.5 milliliters (ml.)
1 tsp.	3/4 tsp.	5 ml.
1 tablespoon (tbsp.) = 3 tsp.	3/4 tbsp.	15 ml.
1 ounce (oz.) = 2 tbsp.	1 ounce	29 ml.
1 cup (c.) = 8 oz., 16 tbsp., 48 tsp.	4/5 cup	237 ml. (approx. 1/4 L.)
1 pint (pt.) = 2 cups	4/5 pt. = 12/3 cups	473 ml. (approx. 1/2 L.)
1 quart (qt.) = 2 pt.	4/5 qt. = 31/3 cups	946 ml. (approx. 1 L.)

TEMPERATURES

$$\text{FAHRENHEIT} = \frac{\text{CELSIUS} \times 9}{5} + 32 \qquad \text{CELSIUS} = \frac{(\text{FAHRENHEIT} - 32) \times 5}{9}$$

100°F.	= 38°C. (37.8°C.)
120°F.	= 49°C. (48.9°C.)
130°F.	= 54°C. (54.4°C.)
140°F.	= 60°C. (60°C.)
150°F.	= 66°C. (65.6°C.)
160°F.	= 71°C. (71.1°C.)
165°F.	= 74°C. (73.9°C.)
170°F.	= 77°C. (76.7°C.)

FAHRENHEIT	CELSIUS	BRITISH GAS NO. (REGULO)
225°F.	= 110°C. (107.2°C.)	= 1/4
250°F.	= 120°C. (121.1°C.)	= 1/2
275°F.	= 135°C. (135°C.)	= 1
300°F.	= 150°C. (148.9°C.)	= 2
325°F	= 163°C. (162.8°C.)	= 3
350°F.	= 175°C. (176.7°C.)	= 4
375°F.	= 190°C. (190.6°C.)	= 5
400°F.	= 205°C. (204.4°C.)	= 6
425°F.	= 220°C. (218.3°C.)	= 7
450°F	= 230°C. (232.2°C.)	= 8

CAN SIZES, APPROXIMATE WEIGHT
AND APPROXIMATE CONTENT IN CUPS (U.S.)

8-ounce can	= 8 ounces	= 1 cup
Picnic	= 10 1/2 to 12 ounces	= 1 1/4 cups
12-ounce can	= 12 ounces	= 1 1/2 cups
No. 300 can	= 14 to 16 ounces	= 1 3/4 cups
No. 303 can	= 16 to 17 ounces	= 2 cups
No. 2 can	= 1 pound, 4 ounces, or 20 ounces	= 2 1/2 cups
No. 2 1/2 can	= 1 pound, 13 ounces, or 29 ounces	= 3 1/2 cups
No. 3 can	= 2 pounds, 14 ounces, or 1 quart, 14 fluid ounces	= 5 3/4 cups

Simple Sauces and Dressings for PASTA

Let's face it, cooking is a chore—even when carried out as a labor of love. On the days you can't bear to look another recipe in the eye, there's comfort in knowing how to feed the family without a fuss. The following simple sauces and pasta dressings are perfect when you need to get dinner on the table quickly. You can store them in the refrigerator for a few days, an extra time-saving perk when you need to prepare dinner in advance. Most sauces freeze well, too.

Although these sauces and dressings are delicious on their own, don't be afraid to incorporate other ingredients from your fridge. Chunks of roast chicken, turkey, or lean beef, or sliced fresh mozzarella cheese, tomatoes, or steamed vegetables—all lend a delicious variation to many pasta sauces and salads. To keep the sauce from cooling down too much, remove all additions from the fridge *before* putting up the water to boil.

Familiarize yourself with traditional pasta and sauce pairings (see pages 5–8), but please don't limit yourself. A good cook requires freedom of choice, as well as common sense. If necessary, replace a different pasta for the one specified in these or any other recipes you feel like cooking.

Basic White Sauce for Pasta

With this sauce in your freezer, pasta quickly turns into a complete meal when you add other ingredients. Cooked peas, spinach, broccoli, cauliflower, bell peppers, carrots, corn, onion, chicken, or baked ham are just a partial list of foods that taste wonderful with white sauce. Add seasonings such as curry, fresh herbs, or prepared mustards, and pasta is suddenly a delicious and satisfying supper. For a light meal, pour white sauce over pasta and add a sprinkling of your favorite cheese. In this recipe, the flour is first lightly toasted to enrich the flavor of the sauce without using more butter.

1/4 CUP UNSIFTED ALL-PURPOSE FLOUR
2 TABLESPOONS BUTTER
4 CUPS LOW-FAT MILK, HEATED
SALT AND FRESHLY GROUND WHITE PEPPER, TO TASTE

MAKES 4 CUPS, ENOUGH FOR ABOUT 2 POUNDS PASTA

1. Over very low heat, toast the flour in a large nonaluminum saucepan, stirring constantly with a whisk or wooden spoon, for 2 minutes, or until barely golden.

2. Add the butter and stir quickly for 1 minute. The lumps in the mixture are okay for now.

3. Increase the heat to medium-high and gradually pour in the hot milk, a few tablespoons at a time, whisking constantly until the sauce is thick and free of lumps, which occurs approximately after 3/4 cup milk has been added. At this point you can add the milk more quickly, but continue to whisk constantly, until the sauce is very thick, completely smooth, and just barely simmering, about 3 minutes.

4. Simmer the sauce over low heat until thoroughly cooked (which means the sauce won't taste like flour), 5 to 6 minutes. Season to taste with salt and pepper. The sauce is ready to use now, or allow the sauce to cool, covered, to room temperature. Pour cooled sauce into containers, seal tightly, and freeze or refrigerate until needed.

Once frozen, don't bother to defrost before using. Just heat sauce over medium heat, and add the other ingredients and seasonings to heat through. Pour over hot pasta.

This sauce keeps in the refrigerator for 4 to 5 days and freezes for up to 2 months.

Note: *Substitute 4 cups chicken broth for the milk. The sauce will be slightly thinner, but still taste quite delicious.*

The Science of Salt

Pick up any number of cookbooks and there's a good chance you'll read conflicting advice about when you should add salt to pasta water—some say before the water boils, others say not until after. Does it matter? Well, yes and no. The answer comes down to this: Salt raises the boiling point of water. Pasta cooked in salted water cooks faster because the water is hotter. The quicker the pasta cooks, the better it tastes. If you add salt beforehand, however, you'll wait longer for the water to come to a boil than if you salt the water afterward. The choice is yours.

Peanut Sauce

This flavorful sauce appeals both to kids and adults.

1/2 CUP CANNED LOW-SODIUM
   CHICKEN BROTH

1/3 CUP CREAMY PEANUT BUTTER,
   PREFERABLY MADE FROM PEANUTS
   ONLY

3 TABLESPOONS REDUCED-SODIUM
   SOY SAUCE

1 TABLESPOON RICE VINEGAR OR
   FRESH LEMON JUICE

2 TEASPOONS SESAME OIL

1/2 TEASPOON CRUSHED RED PEPPER
   FLAKES (OPTIONAL)

MAKES ABOUT 1 CUP, ENOUGH FOR
12 OUNCES COOLED SPAGHETTINI
OR ANGEL HAIR PASTA

In a small bowl, whisk broth and peanut butter into a smooth paste. Add the soy sauce, rice vinegar, sesame oil, and red pepper flakes and whisk until smooth. Toss with cooked pasta.

Note: *Serve with strips of cold roasted chicken and sprinkle with a tablespoon of thinly sliced scallion.*

Pesto Sauce

When basil is abundant and most affordable at the market, it pays to make large batches of pesto. It's easy to make, freezes beautifully (see instructions below), and boosts the flavor of many foods. Pesto is a perfect partner to pasta, but it also mates well with poultry, potato, rice, and other dishes.

There's virtually no work involved when pesto is prepared in a food processor or blender, so you might as well make several batches whenever possible. This recipe can be doubled or tripled with great success.

Omit the Parmesan cheese and pine nuts if you plan to freeze the pesto before using. Add the cheese and nuts after the pesto has thawed and use immediately or refrigerate for up to 1 week.

In a food processor or blender, process the basil, olive oil, pine nuts, garlic, and Parmesan cheese until just smooth, leaving some texture. Season to taste with salt and pepper. Use immediately or refrigerate for up to 1 week.

Note: *Variations: For a lower-fat version, reduce oil to 2 tablespoons, and add 3 tablespoons chicken broth and 2 tablespoons part-skim ricotta cheese. Makes about 2 cups.*

Pesto with vegetables: Cut 2 medium red potatoes into 1/2-inch cubes. Steam potatoes and 4 ounces tender green beans until crisp-tender, 6 to 8 minutes. Toss with hot pasta and pesto.

2 CUPS PACKED FRESH BASIL LEAVES, WASHED AND PATTED DRY

1/3 CUP EXTRA-VIRGIN OLIVE OIL

2 TABLESPOONS PINE NUTS OR COARSELY CHOPPED WALNUTS

2 GARLIC CLOVES, COARSELY CHOPPED

1/3 CUP FRESHLY GRATED PARMESAN CHEESE

SALT AND FRESHLY GROUND BLACK PEPPER, TO TASTE

MAKES ABOUT 2 CUPS, ENOUGH FOR 16 OUNCES PASTA

Pesto Plus

Add a tablespoon or two of pesto to purchased or homemade tomato sauce.

Swirl some pesto on bread and make a sandwich using cold roasted chicken, turkey or ham, adding lettuce and tomato, if you like.

Spread pesto under the skin of chicken before roasting.

Combine the last of the pesto with chicken broth or a mild vinaigrette and serve over steamed vegetables.

Red Salsa Supreme

Salsa, the Spanish word for "sauce," is found all over the super-markets these days—next to corn chips, near taco shells, and stocked in the refrigerator section. Although traditionally used as a condiment, salsa suits pasta remarkably well. Serve this salsa with short, thick pasta such as penne or rigatoni. Alternatively, whirl ingredients in batches in a food processor or blender, leaving some texture to the sauce, and serve over spaghetti or ribbon pasta.

1 POUND RIPE TOMATOES, CORED
   AND CHOPPED
3 SCALLIONS, SLICED
3/4 CUP CHOPPED FRESH CILANTRO
2 GARLIC CLOVES, MINCED OR
   PRESSED
2 TABLESPOONS LEMON OR LIME
   JUICE
1 TEASPOON GROUND CUMIN, CHILI
   POWDER, OR CAYENNE
SALT, TO TASTE

MAKES ENOUGH FOR
16 OUNCES PASTA

Combine tomato, scallions, cilantro, garlic, lemon juice, and ground cumin in a medium bowl and stir to mix. Season to taste with salt. Mixture may stand tightly covered at room temperature for up to 4 hours, or kept in the refrigerator for up to 4 days.

About Cilantro

Cilantro, a leafy herb, is also known as fresh coriander or Chinese parsley. Prized for its unique flavor, cilantro has been considered a favorite among the cuisines of Africa, Asia, India, and Latin America for a long time, while its widespread use in American kitchens is fairly new. Add cilantro to bean dishes, soups, marinades, sauces, salsas, and stews. The chopped fresh leaves and delicate stems should be added at the end of cooking time.

Cut off the leafy top of a bunch of cilantro and discard the thicker stems. Swish the leaves and tender stems several times in a large bowl of cold water. Pat dry with a clean dish towel before chopping. Chop the delicate and delicious upper stems along with the leaves.

Quick Tomato and Veal Sauce

1. Heat oil in a large nonstick skillet over medium-low heat. Add onion and garlic and cook, stirring, until onion softens, about 5 minutes.

2. Crumble the veal into the skillet and cook, stirring occasionally, until meat loses its pink color. Add reserved juices from canned tomatoes and cook until juices almost evaporate. Add puréed tomatoes and oregano and stir to blend. Heat sauce to a gentle boil, then simmer uncovered for 15 minutes. Remove from heat. Season to taste with salt and pepper.

3. To serve, toss with pasta, 2 tablespoons chopped fresh parsley, and Parmesan cheese.

1 TABLESPOON OLIVE OIL
1 SMALL ONION, DICED
2 GARLIC CLOVES, MINCED OR PRESSED
3/4 POUND GROUND VEAL
1 CAN (28 OUNCES) ITALIAN-STYLE PLUM TOMATOES, PURÉED WITHOUT JUICES, JUICES RESERVED
2 TEASPOONS DRIED OREGANO
SALT AND FRESHLY GROUND BLACK PEPPER, TO TASTE
2 TABLESPOONS CHOPPED FRESH PARSLEY
FRESHLY GRATED PARMESAN CHEESE, TO TASTE

MAKES ENOUGH FOR 12 OUNCES PASTA

2 Heads Are Better Than 1 Garlic Sauce

Garlic cloves are delicious and mild tasting when simmered in broth. Serve with any ribbon or medium-to-long tube pasta

2 LARGE HEADS OF GARLIC (OR AS MANY AS YOUR HEART DESIRES)
1 1/2 CUPS CHICKEN OR VEGETABLE BROTH
1/4 CUP MINCED FRESH PARSLEY
1 TEAPOON EXTRA-VIRGIN OLIVE OIL
1/8 TEASPOON CRUSHED RED PEPPER FLAKES, OR TO TASTE
SALT AND FRESHLY GROUND BLACK PEPPER, TO TASTE

MAKES ABOUT 1 CUP, ENOUGH FOR 16 OUNCES PASTA

1. Separate garlic cloves from head. Pull off excess papery skin, leaving cloves covered with a thin layer of peel. Heat cloves and broth in a 2-quart saucepan over high heat until boiling, then lower heat and simmer, partially covered, until cloves are soft, about 20 minutes.

2. Turn off heat and remove any papery garlic skins floating in broth. Stir in parsley, olive oil, crushed red pepper, and salt and pepper to taste. Use immediately, store in refrigerator for up to 3 days, or freeze up to 3 months. (To serve, toss with hot pasta

How to Peel a garlic clove

To peel, first place the clove on a cutting board. Put the flat side of a broad knife on top of the garlic and pound it with your palm. This blow separates the papery skin from the clove for easy removal. Using a microwave oven is great when you need to peel a whole head of garlic. Place the entire head of garlic (or as many cloves as you need) in a microwave-safe dish. Microwave on HIGH (100% power) until garlic softens slightly, 5 to 10 seconds for 1 clove or 45 to 55 seconds for the entire head. Slip off skin with your fingers.

Garlic Sense

A "head" of garlic is generally made up of 10 to 12 individual "cloves." Select firm heads with plump outside cloves that are free of dark spots or sprouting.

Store whole heads of garlic in a cool, dark, well-ventilated spot for up to 8 weeks. Individual cloves, once broken from the head, will keep for up to 10 days.

Crushing, mincing, or pressing garlic releases pungent juices and gives it a more intense flavor than that of garlic that is halved, sliced, or left whole.

Press a clove with peel left on for maximum flavor, as well as easy cleanup. The papery skin permits the mashed garlic and its oil to pass through the tiny holes unhindered, and you can pull out the paper skin freely with your fingers.

When you have no choice but to use sprouted garlic, cut the clove in half and remove and discard the center-green-colored shoot.

1 medium garlic clove equals 1/2 teaspoon minced or pressed garlic. Fresh garlic is always preferred to prepared garlic, which you can buy in jars from the supermarket. In a real pinch, you can substitute 1/8 teaspoon garlic powder or instant minced garlic.

Roasted Peppers and Garlic Sauce

You can prepare and refrigerate this flavorful sauce up to two days ahead, but bring to room temperature before serving over hot pasta.

2 POUNDS (ABOUT 7) MEDIUM BELL
   PEPPERS, RED, YELLOW, OR ANY
   MIX OF THE TWO
3 GARLIC CLOVES, MINCED OR
   PRESSED
2 TABLESPOONS OLIVE OIL
2 TABLESPOONS BALSAMIC VINEGAR
1/4 TEASPOON SALT
PINCH OF CRUSHED RED PEPPER
   FLAKES (OPTIONAL)

MAKES ABOUT 3 CUPS,
ENOUGH FOR 16 OUNCES PASTA

1. Preheat broiler. Cut the bell peppers in half lengthwise and discard the seeds and membranes. Place pepper halves, skin side up, on a foil-lined baking sheet and flatten with palm of hand. Broil for 12 minutes, or until blackened and charred. Place the peppers in a tightly covered bowl or seal in a zip-top, heavy-duty plastic bag. Let peppers cool for 15 minutes. Set aside any pan drippings.

2. Peel and discard the skins. Cut the bell peppers into thin strips.

3. Combine the bell pepper strips, pan drippings, garlic, oil, and vinegar in a medium bowl and toss thoroughly. Add salt and red pepper flakes. Use immediately or refrigerate in a closed container for up to 2 days. To serve, toss with pasta and Parmesan cheese.

☆ SAUCE AND DRESSING PROPORTIONS

The quantity of sauce or dressing for each portion of pasta depends on the type of sauce or dressing itself. Use the amounts given here as a guide to help you determine how much sauce you really need.

SAUCES

THIN SAUCES:
1/4 TO 1/3 CUP PER POUND OF PASTA

THICK SMOOTH SAUCES:
1/2 TO 3/4 CUP PER POUND OF PASTA

PURÉED SAUCES:
1 TO 1 1/2 CUPS PER POUND OF PASTA

CHUNKY SAUCES:
2 TO 4 CUPS PER POUND OF PASTA

DRESSINGS

ONE POUND OF COOKED PASTA
NEEDS 1/2 TO 3/4 CUP OF A THIN DRESSING

ONE POUND OF COOKED PASTA
NEEDS 3/4 TO 1 CUP OF A THICKER DRESSING

Double-Red Pasta Sauce

Spike this mildly sweet sauce with balsamic vinegar when you want a tangier taste.

1 JAR (7 OUNCES) ROASTED RED
    PEPPERS, RINSED AND WELL
    DRAINED
2 MEDIUM-SIZE RIPE TOMATOES
3 TABLESPOONS OLIVE OIL
2 TABLESPOONS FRESHLY GRATED
    PARMESAN CHEESE
1 GARLIC CLOVE, MINCED OR PRESSED
2 TABLESPOONS MINCED FRESH
    PARSLEY
1/4 TEASPOON DRIED OREGANO
SALT AND FRESHLY GROUND BLACK
    PEPPER, TO TASTE
1 TABLESPOON BALSAMIC VINEGAR
    OR LEMON JUICE (OPTIONAL)

MAKES ABOUT 1 1/2 CUPS SAUCE,
ENOUGH FOR 16 OUNCES PASTA

Purée red peppers, tomatoes, olive oil, and Parmesan cheese in a food processor until smooth. Stir in garlic, parsley, and oregano. Add salt and pepper to taste. If you like, add balsamic vinegar. Store covered in the refrigerator for up to 2 days. Bring to room temperature before using. Toss with warm or room temperature pasta.

Versatile Vinaigrette Dressing

*This recipe cures the "practically empty cupboard syndrome,"
when there's nothing but this dressing and a box of pasta in the
house. Best of all, the dressing tastes great with just about any
pasta salad.*

Combine the Dijon mustard, water, vinegar, and garlic in a small
jar with tight-fitting lid. Shake vigorously to combine. Add the oil
and shake again until smooth. Season to taste with salt and
pepper. Store, covered, in the refrigerator for up to 2 weeks.
Shake well before using.

2 TEASPOONS DIJON MUSTARD
4 TABLESPOONS WATER
1/2 CUP RED OR WHITE WINE
  VINEGAR
1 LARGE GARLIC CLOVE, MINCED OR
  PRESSED
1/3 CUP EXTRA-VIRGIN OLIVE OIL
SALT AND FRESHLY GROUND BLACK
  PEPPER, TO TASTE

MAKES ABOUT 1 1/2 CUPS,
ENOUGH FOR 2 POUNDS PASTA

Citrus Salad Dressing

This delicious dressing works particularly well with pasta salads containing canned tuna, tomatoes, bell peppers, and feta cheese, but it's also delicious when paired with poultry and/or vegetable pasta salads.

1/3 CUP EXTRA-VIRGIN OLIVE OIL

1/3 CUP ORANGE JUICE

2 TO 3 GARLIC CLOVES, MINCED OR PRESSED

3 TABLESPOONS VINEGAR OR LEMON JUICE

1 TABLESPOON CAPERS, RINSED AND DRAINED

1/2 TEASPOON DRIED OREGANO, OR 1 TABLESPOON MINCED FRESH HERBS, SUCH AS MINT OR PARSLEY

SALT AND FRESHLY GROUND BLACK PEPPER, TO TASTE

MAKES ABOUT 3/4 CUP, ENOUGH FOR 16 OUNCES PASTA

Combine the olive oil, orange juice, garlic, vinegar, capers, and oregano in a small jar with a tight-fitting lid. Shake vigorously to combine. Season to taste with salt and pepper and store, covered, in the refrigerator for up to 3 days.

Creamy Garlic Dressing

Whisk together all ingredients in a small mixing bowl. Refrigerate in a covered jar and use within 3 days.

1 CUP PLAIN LOW-FAT YOGURT

2 TABLESPOONS LOW-FAT MILK

2 TABLESPOONS CHOPPED FRESH PARSLEY, OR 1 TEASPOON DRIED CHERVIL OR OREGANO

2 TO 3 GARLIC CLOVES, MINCED OR PRESSED

2 TEASPOONS VINEGAR

2 TEASPOONS DIJON MUSTARD

1 TEASPOON SUGAR

MAKES ABOUT 1 1/2 CUPS, ENOUGH FOR 1 1/2 POUNDS PASTA

Asian Vinaigrette

This recipe tastes great in salads and also makes a quick dipping sauce for steamed vegetables.

1/4 CUP SEASONED RICE VINEGAR
2 TABLESPOONS CANOLA OR
    VEGETABLE OIL
2 TABLESPOONS SOY SAUCE
1 TEASPOON MINCED FRESH GINGER
2 TEASPOONS HONEY (OPTIONAL)
1 GARLIC CLOVE, MINCED OR PRESSED
2 TABLESPOONS CHOPPED SCALLION

MAKES ABOUT 1/2 CUP, ENOUGH
FOR 8 OUNCES PASTA

Combine all ingredients in a small jar with a tight-fitting lid. Shake vigorously to combine. Store covered in the refrigerator for 1 hour to blend flavors, or up to 2 days. Bring to room temperature before using.

Note: *Pasta combo: Serve with thin pasta strands, strips of cold roasted chicken, and snow peas. Sprinkle with sesame seeds.*

Creamy Herb Dressing

This tangy low-fat dressing tastes great with pasta salads containing poultry or vegetables.

In a medium bowl, whisk together buttermilk, mayonnaise, water, lemon juice, garlic, chervil, and pepper until smooth. Cover and refrigerate for 30 minutes to allow flavors to blend, or up to 3 days. Remove just before you boil the water for the pasta.

3/4 CUP BUTTERMILK

1/3 CUP LIGHT MAYONNAISE

1/4 CUP WATER

1 TABLESPOON LEMON JUICE OR
   VINEGAR

1 GARLIC CLOVE, MINCED OR PRESSED

1 TEASPOON DRIED CHERVIL, OREGANO,
   OR TARRAGON

1/4 TEASPOON FRESHLY GROUND BLACK
   PEPPER

MAKES ABOUT 1 1/4 CUPS,
ENOUGH FOR 16 OUNCES PASTA

Roasted Garlic

When garlic is roasted, the flavor becomes sweet and slightly nutty, and the texture is buttery soft. Select fat bulbs for roasting. Each roasted head will yield roughly 1/4 cup of mashed garlic pulp. You can substitute it for minced raw garlic in pasta sauces, salsas, salad dressings, and any recipe in which you might prefer a more mellow taste of garlic.

3 LARGE GARLIC HEADS
1 TABLESPOON EXTRA-VIRGIN OLIVE
  OIL
FRESHLY GROUND BLACK PEPPER

SERVES 4 TO 6

1. Cut off the flat end of each garlic head to expose whole cloves. Spread cloves apart, keeping tight outer papery skin intact. Trim pointed end so heads will sit flat. Place heads, trimmed end down, in a small baking dish or on a sheet of aluminum foil. Drizzle heads with olive oil and sprinkle with pepper. Cover with a lid or wrap in foil.

2. Bake at 350°F for 1 hour, or until heads are golden and cloves are very soft. Cool. Squeeze out pulp from each individual clove. If not using immediately, refrigerate in covered container.

Note: *Roasted Garlic Spread: In a food processor or blender, whirl together 1/4 cup roasted garlic pulp with 2 tablespoons extra-virgin olive oil. Add 8 ounces reduced-fat cream cheese, softened, 1/4 cup chopped fresh herbs, such as parsley, basil, or dill, and whirl until smooth. Season to taste with salt and freshly ground pepper. Cover and refrigerate for up to 5 days. Serve spread with pita wedges, bagel chips, or toasted French baguette slices. Makes about 1 3/4 cups.*

Roasted Garlic Sauce for Pasta: Add milk to Roasted Garlic Spread to desired consistency and toss with hot cooked pasta.

Quick PASTA from the Pantry

When there's nothing but the bare essentials in the fridge, a pantry packed with canned food and pasta can come to your rescue. It's so ridiculously easy to pull together a meal with tuna, clams, beans, or tomatoes that you may want to rely on pantry dishes often. Stay on top of what you use up by making a shopping list of each item you use the *moment* you use it. Replace them A.S.A.P.

Spicy Black Bean and Tomato Sauce

This sauce tastes delicious with or without fresh cilantro leaves.

1 TABLESPOON OLIVE OIL

2 GARLIC CLOVES, MINCED OR PRESSED

1 TEASPOON CHILI POWDER

1 TEASPOON GROUND CUMIN

1 CAN (14 1/2 OUNCES) MEXICAN-STYLE TOMATOES, OR STEWED TOMATOES

1 CAN (15 TO 19 OUNCES) BLACK BEANS

12 OUNCES ROTINI, FUSILLI, OR ROTELLE

1/2 CUP PACKED FRESH CILANTRO

SERVES 3-4

1. Combine oil and garlic in a large nonstick skillet. Cook and stir over medium heat until garlic releases its aroma, about 1 minute. Add the chili powder and ground cumin and stir constantly for 1 minute. Add the tomatoes and beans, breaking up the tomatoes with the back of a spoon while stirring the sauce. When sauce begins to boil, lower the heat, cover, and simmer for 20 minutes. Remove from heat.

2. While sauce simmers, bring 4 quarts of water to a boil in a large covered pot. Add 2 teaspoons salt, if you like. Add pasta, stir, and partially cover the pot until water returns to a boil. Immediately remove cover, stir again, and cook pasta just until al dente. Drain water from pasta and return to covered pot, off the heat, if sauce is not ready.

3. Add pasta to sauce. Add fresh cilantro. Over low heat, lift with tongs or two forks and toss to coat for 1 minute.

Spaghetti With Tuna and Spicy Red Sauce

You can make this dish with tuna packed in oil or water. If packed in water, use 1 tablespoon olive oil in step 3.

1. Bring 4 quarts of water to a boil in a large covered pot. Add 2 teaspoons salt, if you like. Add pasta, stir, and partially cover the pot until water returns to a boil. Immediately remove cover, stir again, and cook pasta just until al dente. Drain water from pasta and return to covered pot, off the heat, if sauce is not ready.

2. Drain tuna, reserving 1 tablespoon oil. Put tuna in a small bowl and flake the tuna with a fork.

3. Heat the reserved oil and garlic in a medium nonstick skillet over medium heat for 1 minute, stirring constantly, until garlic releases its aroma. Add puréed tomatoes, reserved juices, olives, capers, red pepper flakes, and 3 tablespoons parsley. Stir to mix. Heat to boiling, then reduce heat and simmer over low heat, uncovered, for 15 minutes, until slightly thickened. Remove from heat.

4. Add sauce to pasta. Over low heat, lift with tongs or two forks to coat for 1 minute. Remove from heat. Gently toss in tuna. Sprinkle with remaining parsley and serve at once.

12 OUNCES SPAGHETTI

1 CAN (6 1/2 OUNCES) ITALIAN TUNA

3 GARLIC CLOVES, MINCED OR PRESSED

1 CAN (28 OUNCES) ITALIAN-STYLE PLUM TOMATOES, PURÉED WITHOUT JUICES, JUICES RESERVED

1/3 CUP BRINE-PACKED BLACK OLIVES, PITTED AND CHOPPED

2 TABLESPOONS CAPERS, DRAINED AND RINSED

1/4 TEASPOON CRUSHED RED PEPPER FLAKES, OR TO TASTE

4 TABLESPOONS CHOPPED FRESH PARSLEY

SERVES 4

4 1

Pasta With Fennel and Sardines

The natural sweetness of fennel tastes like licorice and is available throughout the winter months.

12 OUNCES SPAGEHETTI

2 TABLESPOONS OLIVE OIL

1 CUP CHOPPED ONION

1 LARGE FENNEL BULB (ABOUT 3/4 POUND) TRIMMED AND THINLY SLICED (SEE NOTE)

2 CUPS CHICKEN BROTH OR CANNED LOW-SODIUM BROTH

2 TABLESPOONS LIGHT OR DARK RAISINS OR CURRANTS

SALT AND FRESHLY GROUND BLACK PEPPER, TO TASTE

2 CANS (4 1/2 OUNCES EACH) SARDINES PACKED IN WATER, DRAINED

2 TABLESPOONS CHOPPED FRESH PARSLEY

SERVES 4

1. Bring 4 quarts of water to a boil in a large covered pot. Add 2 teaspoons salt, if you like. Add pasta, stir, and partially cover the pot until water returns to a boil. Immediately remove cover, stir again, and cook pasta just until al dente. Drain water from pasta and return to covered pot, off the heat, if sauce is not ready.

2. While pasta cooks, heat oil in a medium nonstick skillet over medium-low heat. Add onion and fennel. Cook for about 10 minutes, stirring occasionally, until onion is soft and translucent and fennel is crisp-tender. Add chicken broth and raisins. Raise heat to medium high and gently simmer, uncovered, for 3 to 4 minutes. Season to taste with salt and pepper.

3. Add the sauce to the pasta and toss over low heat, for 30 seconds, until heated through. Add sardines and parsley and gently toss again. Serve immediately.

Note: *Trim the stalks off the fennel bulb and cut away any bruised, discolored, or tough outer leaves. Cut the fennel bulb in half lengthwise. Trim the root end and cut the core at the base of the bulb. Slice the fennel lengthwise into thin strips.*

Fennel Facts

Fennel is a bulb-shaped vegetable that has the texture of celery, the taste of licorice, and the feathery greens of fresh dill! When cooked, it becomes deliciously sweet but not cloying. For a sensational treat, drizzle a little extra-virgin olive oil and lemon juice over slivers of raw fennel and serve as a first course. Fennel is available from October through May.

Linguine With Red Clam Sauce

1. Bring 4 quarts of water to a boil in a large covered pot. Add 2 teaspoons salt, if you like. Add pasta, stir, and partially cover the pot until water returns to a boil. Immediately remove cover, stir again, and cook pasta just until al dente. Drain water from pasta and return to covered pot, off the heat, if sauce is not ready.

2. While pasta cooks, drain juices from minced clams into a measuring cup, reserving the minced clams. Add enough bottled clam juice to make 1 1/2 cups. Warm oil and garlic in a large skillet over medium heat, stirring, until garlic begins to color, about 2 minutes. Immediately remove skillet from heat. Add clam juice, tomatoes, parsley, thyme, and red pepper flakes. Stir well and add salt and pepper to taste. Return skillet to low heat and cook sauce for 6 to 8 minutes, uncovered. Remove from heat.

3. Add pasta and reserved clams to sauce. Over low heat, lift with tongs or two forks and toss to coat for 1 minute. Serve immediately.

16 OUNCES LINGUINE

3 CANS (6 1/2 OUNCES EACH) MINCED CLAMS

BOTTLED CLAM JUICE

2 TABLESPOONS OLIVE OIL

2 LARGE GARLIC CLOVES, MINCED OR PRESSED

1 CAN (14 OUNCES) STEWED OR PURÉED TOMATOES

2 TABLESPOONS FINELY CHOPPED FRESH PARSLEY

1 TEASPOON DRIED THYME

1/8 TEASPOON CRUSHED RED PEPPER FLAKES

SALT AND FRESHLY GROUND BLACK PEPPER, TO TASTE

SERVES 4

Pasta With Chick-peas, Tomatoes, and Rosemary

Asiago cheese is sharp, nutty cow's milk cheese that tastes superb grated over pasta dishes. It is saltier than Parmesan, so you may want to use less than usual.

12 OUNCES PENNE OR MEDIUM
    TUBULAR PASTA
1 CAN (28 OUNCES) ITALIAN-STYLE
    PLUM TOMATOES, JUICES DRAINED
    AND RESERVED
2 GARLIC CLOVES, MINCED OR PRESSED
1 CAN (14 OUNCES) CHICK-PEAS, RINSED
    AND DRAINED
1 TEASPOON DRIED ROSEMARY
1/2 CUP FINELY GRATED ASIAGO OR
    PARMESAN CHEESE

SERVES 4 TO 6

1. Bring 4 quarts of water to a boil in a large covered pot. Add 2 teaspoons salt, if you like. Add pasta, stir, and partially cover the pot until water returns to a boil. Immediately remove cover, stir again, and cook pasta just until al dente. Drain water from pasta and return to covered pot, off the heat, if sauce is not ready.

2. While pasta cooks, gently simmer reserved tomato juices and garlic in a large uncovered skillet over low heat for 5 minutes, until garlic begins to soften. Add chick-peas and mash half with a potato masher or back of a large spoon. Cook, stirring occasionally, for 5 minutes, until heated through. Add tomatoes and rosemary. Bring mixture to a boil over medium-high heat, stirring and breaking up tomatoes with spoon. Reduce heat to medium low. Simmer, uncovered, for 10 minutes, until sauce thickens slightly. Remove from heat.

3. Add pasta to sauce. Over low heat, lift with tongs or two forks and toss to coat for 1 minute. Add grated cheese and toss gently. Serve immediately.

Linguine With Herbed Crumbs

This makes a great late-night snack.

1. Bring 4 quarts of water to a boil in a large covered pot. Add 2 teaspoons salt, if you like. Add pasta, stir, and partially cover the pot until water returns to a boil. Immediately remove cover, stir again, and cook pasta just until al dente. Drain water from pasta and return to pot, off the heat. Add broth to pasta and toss well.

2. While pasta cooks, heat oil in a large nonstick skillet over medium heat. Add bread crumbs, garlic, basil, and parsley and cook, stirring constantly, for 4 to 5 minutes, until crumbs are golden and crisp.

3. Add crumb mixture and salt and pepper to pasta. Over low heat, lift with tongs or two forks and toss to coat for 1 minute. Serve immediately.

12 OUNCES LINGUINE

3 TABLESPOONS CHICKEN OR VEGETABLE BROTH

2 TABLESPOONS EXTRA-VIRGIN OLIVE OIL

2 CUPS COARSE BREAD CRUMBS

2 LARGE GARLIC CLOVES, MINCED OR PRESSED

1/4 CUP FINELY CHOPPED FRESH BASIL

1/4 CUP MINCED FRESH PARSLEY

SALT AND FRESHLY GROUND BLACK PEPPER, TO TASTE

SERVES 4

PASTA

Soups

Ladle a bowl full of steaming soup and you're sure to cut the chill on a frosty day. By joining little more than broth, leftover steamed vegetables, and cooked beans, you can develop delicious soups from scratch. Season your soups with different spice combinations, and suddenly an endless variety of pasta soups becomes possible.

Choose small pasta shapes or narrow strands for thin, brothlike soups. Thicker and medium-size pasta shapes are best suited for chunky soups chock-full with beans, vegetables, poultry, or meat.

Chicken Broth

My dear friend Lorna Vanterpool taught me an easy way to skim off the majority of fat before adding other ingredients. Carrots galore contribute a mild, sweet flavor to this terrific chicken broth. Serve over any pasta noodle, or use in soups or as an ingredient in sauces.

1 WHOLE CHICKEN, ABOUT 3 1/2
    POUNDS
1 LARGE ONION, UNPEELED,
    QUARTERED
6 LARGE CARROTS, SCRUBBED AND CUT
    INTO 2-INCH LENGTHS
3 PARSLEY SPRIGS
2 CELERY STALKS, CUT INTO 2-INCH
    LENGTHS
1 TEASPOON SALT

MAKES ABOUT **2 1/2** QUARTS

1. Rinse chicken very well in cold water and remove any clumps of blood found in the cavity. Cut chicken skin at base of neck with kitchen scissors or a knife, and using a kitchen towel, get a good grip on the skin and pull off as much as possible, and discard. Cut chicken in half down backbone and through breast.

2. Put chicken halves in a stockpot or Dutch oven. Add enough cold water to cover by about 3 inches and heat to a boil. When water boils, reduce heat and simmer, and use a large spoon or ladle to skim off as much fat as possible. The fat will accumulate around the side of the pot, making removal easy. This takes about 5 minutes. Add onion, carrots, parsley, and celery and return to a boil. Reduce the heat and simmer, partially covered, for 2 hours. Skim fat as necessary. Add salt midway through cooking.

3. Transfer chicken to a bowl and cool, leaving behind any bones that may have fallen from the chicken. When cool, pull meat from bones and squeeze out the liquid. Put the bones and liquid in the broth. Discard the meat.

4. Strain broth. Press the bones and vegetables firmly to force out all the liquid. Skim fat if necessary. If not using broth immediately, refrigerate, covered, for up to 3 days, or freeze.

 TIME SAVER

Peeling onions for stock or broth is wasted energy. Cut off the root end if it's dirty, but leave the skin intact. In fact, chefs confess to leaving the skin on not only to save time, but also to help color the stock. Ditto for peeling carrots, although they do require scrubbing before taking the plunge.

Vegetable Broth

You can use this light broth as an alternative to beef or chicken broth.

1. Put all ingredients except salt in a large stockpot or Dutch oven. Add enough cold water to cover the ingredients by 1 inch. Bring to a boil. Reduce the heat and simmer, partially covered, for 1 hour. Add salt midway through cooking.

2. Strain broth. Press the vegetables firmly to force out all the liquid. Discard vegetables. If not using broth immediately, refrigerate, covered, for up to a week, or freeze.

3 CELERY STALKS, WITH LEAVES, CHOPPED

4 CARROTS, SCRUBBED AND CHOPPED

3 PARSNIPS OR TURNIPS, TRIMMED, SCRUBBED, AND CHOPPED

3 LEEKS, SPLIT AND CLEANED

3 OR 4 GARLIC CLOVES, UNPEELED, LIGHTLY CRUSHED

2 BAY LEAVES, CRUMBLED

1 LARGE ONION, UNPEELED, ROOT END REMOVED, QUARTERED

1 SMALL BUNCH PARSLEY SPRIGS

1 TEASPOON DRIED THYME

1 TEASPOON DRIED DILL

1 TEASPOON PEPPERCORNS

1 TEASPOON SALT

MAKES ABOUT
2 1/2 QUARTS

Curried Vegetable Soup with Couscous

A tasty, super easy soup to prepare on a moment's notice. Use vegetable broth for a vegetarian delight.

1 TABLESPOON OLIVE OIL

1 MEDIUM ONION, FINELY DICED

3 MEDIUM CARROTS, PEELED AND FINELY DICED

2 MEDIUM ALL-PURPOSE POTATOES, PEELED AND FINELY DICED

2 TABLESPOONS CURRY POWDER

2 CUPS WATER

2 CANS (13 3/4 OUNCES EACH) LOW-SODIUM CHICKEN OR VEGETABLE BROTH

1/2 CUP COUSCOUS

1 1/2 CUPS PLAIN NONFAT YOGURT

2 TABLESPOONS MINCED FRESH CILANTRO OR PARSLEY

SERVES 6

1. Heat oil in a 4-quart saucepan over low heat. Add onion, carrots, and potatoes. Cook, for 8 to 10 minutes, stirring occasionally, until onion turns golden and vegetables are tender. Add curry powder and cook, stirring constantly, for 1 minute. Stir in water and broth. Raise heat and bring mixture to a boil. Reduce heat, cover, and simmer for 10 minutes. Stir in couscous, cover, and cook 6 minutes longer. Remove from heat.

2. In a small bowl, stir together yogurt and 1 or 2 tablespoons hot soup. Keep adding 2 tablespoons soup—yogurt curdles if too much soup is added at once—until yogurt warms through. Slowly add yogurt mixture to soup. Cook over low heat for 1 to 2 minutes, stirring constantly, until completely heated through. *Do not boil soup.* Stir in cilantro and serve at once.

Make the Most of Leftovers

Cover and refrigerate leftover soup, and eat within a day or two. Add additional liquid (broth, water, or vegetable juice) before you reheat, since the soup will thicken while being stored. Stir the soup constantly while heating to prevent solids from sinking to the bottom and scorching.

Enliven the flavor of leftover soup by adding a fresh and different ingredient, such as cooked vegetables or poultry. You could also try adding a few drops of Tabasco, soy sauce, or a teaspoon or two of prepared mustard to pick up the flavor. Another alternative involves reheating the soup and then scattering the top with chopped fresh herbs.

Don't freeze pasta soups. The pasta continues to absorb liquid when cold, creating soggy, tasteless clumps. You may, however, prepare the soup base (minus the pasta) and freeze until needed. Just thaw and reheat the base, adding the uncooked pasta after the base comes to a boil.

Gazpacho with Shells

Dice the vegetables uniformly for this spicy soup.

1. Combine tomatoes, cucumber, onion, bell pepper, and cilantro in a large bowl and mix well. Add tomato juice, lime juice, and garlic and stir to mix. Stir in 2 to 3 drops of Tabasco, or to taste. Cover and refrigerate until well chilled.

2. When ready to serve, bring 4 quarts of water to a boil in a large covered pot. Add 2 teaspoons salt, if you like. Add pasta, stir, and partially cover the pot until water returns to a boil. Immediately remove cover, stir again, and cook pasta just until al dente. Drain the water from the pasta. Plunge pasta into cool water to stop the cooking. Drain again.

3. Ladle gazpacho into 4 chilled soup bowls and top evenly with pasta. Garnish with cilantro leaves.

2 CUPS DICED RIPE PLUM TOMATOES
1/2 CUP DICED CUCUMBER, PEELED
    AND SEEDED
1/2 CUP DICED RED ONION
1 MEDIUM GREEN BELL PEPPER, DICED
3 TABLESPOONS CHOPPED FRESH
    CILANTRO
2 CUPS COLD TOMATO JUICE
2 TABLESPOONS LIME JUICE
2 GARLIC CLOVES, MINCED OR PRESSED
TABASCO SAUCE, TO TASTE
1/2 CUP SMALL PASTA SHELLS
CILANTRO LEAVES, FOR GARNISH

SERVES 4

51

Tortellini and Gremolata in Broth

Gremolata is a mixture of minced garlic, fresh parsley leaves, and lemon peel that cooks traditionally toss into rich Italian sauces to add a fresh light taste. Here, the flavor of the broth simply gets a boost.

6 CUPS CHICKEN OR VEGETABLE BROTH
   (PAGES 48, 49), OR CANNED
   LOW-SODIUM BROTH
1 SMALL CARROT, PEELED AND CUT
   INTO THIN COINS
1 PACKAGE (9 OR 10 OUNCES) FRESH
   CHEESE TORTELLINI
1/4 CUP MINCED FRESH PARSLEY
1 TABLESPOON MINCED GARLIC
2 TABLESPOONS MINCED LEMON PEEL

SERVES 6

1. Bring broth with carrot to a boil in a large covered pot. Add tortellini, reduce heat, and simmer, uncovered, stirring occasionally. Cook tortellini just until al dente.

2. Meanwhile, to make gremolata, mince parsley, garlic, and lemon peel in a food processor or by hand.

3. To serve, ladle simmering soup into bowls and stir about 1 teaspoon gremolata into each serving.

Parsley Power

Common wisdom holds that Italian flat-leaf parsley punches more flavor into food than its curly-leaf cousin, but common sense shouts out that *only the freshest parsley available should be used at all times*. When you select parsley, remember that flavor varies more between individual bunches of parsley than between varieties. Make sure the parsley you choose smells fresh and shows no signs of drooping or yellowing leaves.

To store parsley, pinch off the bottom leaves and place stems in a glass or jar. Add cold water to cover stems by about 1 inch, then cover the parsley loosely with a plastic bag. Keep refrigerated and change the water every 2 days.

52

Buckwheat Noodles with chicken, Snow Peas, and Miso Soup

1. Brush soy sauce on chicken breasts. In a small saucepan, over low heat, bring 1 cup chicken broth to a simmer. Add chicken breasts, cover, and simmer until cooked through, about 8 minutes. Remove chicken from saucepan and cut into thin strips.

2. Strain cooking broth into a medium saucepan. Add miso and stir to mix until thoroughly blended. Add remaining broth and cook over medium-low heat just until broth gently simmers, about 10 minutes. Remove from heat.

3. Meanwhile, bring 4 quarts of water to a boil in a large covered pot. Add noodles and cook until al dente, about 5 minutes. Just before noodles are done, add snow peas and cook for about 45 seconds. Drain water from noodles and snow peas.

4. To serve, mound noodles and snow peas in the center of 4 soup bowls. Top with chicken and sprinkle with scallions. Ladle hot miso soup into each bowl. Serve immediately.

1 TEASPOON LOW-SODIUM SOY SAUCE

1/2 POUND BONELESS, SKINLESS CHICKEN BREASTS

5 CUPS CHICKEN BROTH (PAGE 48), OR CANNED LOW-SODIUM BROTH

1 1/2 TEASPOONS MISO

8 OUNCES BUCKWHEAT NOODLES

1/3 CUP CHINESE SNOW PEAS, TRIMMED AND JULIENNED

3 SCALLIONS, GREEN AND WHITE PARTS, THINLY SLICED

SERVES 4

Miso Paste

Miso is made from fermented soybeans and grains (usually rice or barley), and has a consistency similar to that of peanut butter. Miso tastes salty and, like regular table salt, it brings out the flavor in food. More important, it provides protein and B vitamins to your diet.

Spread miso on sandwiches or use as a seasoning in dressings, soups, and stews. Do not boil miso, because boiling destroys its healthful properties. To substitute miso for salt, use about 1 level tablespoon miso for 1/2 teaspoon salt. Just before serving, whisk miso with a few tablespoons of water in a small bowl to blend, then stir it thoroughly into hot soup, stews, or broth. Miso keeps indefinitely in the refrigerator.

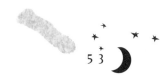

Pasta, Bean, and Escarole Soup

This soup makes a quick, delicious, and filling lunch. Serve with warm, crusty bread.

1/2 CUP CHOPPED ONION

4 CUPS CHICKEN OR VEGETABLE BROTH (PAGES 48, 49), OR CANNED LOW-SODIUM BROTH

1 LARGE GARLIC CLOVE, MINCED OR PRESSED

1 CAN (14 OUNCES) ITALIAN-STYLE PLUM TOMATOES, UNDRAINED

2 CANS (19 OUNCES EACH) WHITE KIDNEY BEANS, RINSED THOROUGHLY UNDER COLD WATER AND DRAINED

1/2 CUP PEELED, DICED CARROT

1 BAY LEAF

1/2 CUP SMALL PASTA SHELLS, DITALINI, OR ELBOWS

2 CUPS PACKED COARSELY CHOPPED FRESH ESCAROLE, KALE, OR SPINACH

FRESHLY GRATED PARMESAN CHEESE

SERVES 4

1. In a 4-quart covered saucepan, cook onion and 1/4 cup broth over low heat, stirring occasionally, until onion is tender, about 5 minutes. Add garlic and cook 1 minute longer.

2. Add remaining broth, tomatoes, beans, carrot, and bay leaf. Raise heat to high and bring mixture to a boil, stirring occasionally. Cover and simmer over low heat for 10 minutes.

3. Stir in pasta and escarole and cook, covered, for 10 to 12 minutes, or until escarole and pasta are tender. Ladle into soup bowls and sprinkle with Parmesan cheese.

★ When Counting Calories Counts

Discard the fat floating in canned broth to eliminate extra calories. Either scoop out fat with a small spoon or pour the broth through a fine-meshed strainer before combining with other ingredients.

Wonton Soup

This recipe is quickly assembled and the wontons cook in less than 2 minutes. The skins should look slightly opaque when done. They will continue to cook in the steaming soup.

1. Bring 4 quarts of water to a boil in a large covered pot.

2. Meanwhile, whirl shrimp, 1 egg white, soy sauce, scallions, garlic, and ginger in a blender or food processor until finely chopped. Lightly beat the remaining egg white in a small bowl.

3. Spread wonton skins on work surface. Place 1 teaspoon of filling in center of each skin. Brush edges with beaten egg white and fold skin diagonally to form a triangle. Press edges to seal, pressing out air. Join two bottom points, one over the other, again forming a triangle, and seal with egg white.

4. Drop wontons into the rapidly boiling water. Return water to a boil and cook wontons for 1 to 2 minutes, or until they are opaque.

5. Remove wontons with a slotted spoon and add to steaming hot, seasoned chicken broth. Stir in sliced scallion greens and serve immediately.

8 OUNCES COOKED, SHELLED, AND
    DEVEINED SHRIMP

2 EGG WHITES

2 TEASPOONS LOW-SODIUM SOY SAUCE

2 SCALLIONS, WHITE PART ONLY,
    COARSELY CHOPPED (RESERVE
    GREEN PART)

1/2 TEASPOON FINELY CHOPPED
    GARLIC

1/2 TEASPOON FINELY CHOPPED
    FRESH GINGER

20 WONTON SKINS (3-INCH SQUARES)

4 CUPS STEAMING HOT CHICKEN BROTH
    (PAGE 48), OR CANNED LOW-
    SODIUM BROTH, SEASONED WITH
    SOY SAUCE TO TASTE

1/4 CUP THINLY SLICED SCALLIONS,
    GREEN PART ONLY

SERVES 4

Chinese-Style Hot and Sour Soup

This flavorful soup needs only a drop or two of chili oil.

8 MEDIUM DRIED SHIITAKE MUSH-
ROOMS (ABOUT 3/4 OUNCE)

3 TABLESPOONS CORNSTARCH

2 TABLESPOONS CANOLA OR
VEGETABLE OIL

1/4 CUP CHOPPED SCALLIONS,
WHITE AND GREEN PARTS

1 TABLESPOON MINCED FRESH
GINGER

3 TABLESPOONS SEASONED RICE
VINEGAR

10 CUPS CHICKEN OR VEGETABLE
BROTH (PAGES 48, 49), OR
CANNED LOW-SODIUM BROTH

3 OUNCES CAPELLINI, BROKEN INTO
2-INCH PIECES, ABOUT 1 CUP

1 POUND TOFU, RINSED, DRAINED,
AND CUT INTO 1/2-INCH CUBES

2 TEASPOONS SOY SAUCE, OR TO
TASTE

CHILI OIL, TO TASTE

SERVES 6 TO 8

1. In a small bowl, soak mushrooms in just enough boiling water to cover for 20 minutes. Remove mushrooms with a slotted spoon. Cut off stems and discard. Cut caps into thin strips and set aside. Strain mushroom liquid and reserve. Rinse and dry bowl.

2. In the same bowl, combine cornstarch with 1/4 cup strained mushroom liquid and stir until smooth. Set aside.

3. Heat oil in a 4- to 5-quart saucepan over medium-high heat. Add scallions and ginger. Cook for 10 to 15 seconds, stirring constantly to prevent scorching. Stir in rice vinegar and cook for 5 seconds. Quickly add broth and mushrooms and heat to boiling. Stir in pasta. Reduce heat and simmer gently for 5 to 7 minutes, until pasta is barely tender and still firm to the bite. Add cornstarch mixture and stir for 45 minutes. Add tofu and soy sauce. Cook over medium-high heat for 2 to 3 minutes, stirring occasionally. When soup starts to boil and thickens slightly, remove from heat. Stir in 1 to 2 drops of chili oil. Offer more oil on the side.

How to Strain Soaking Liquid

Put a paper coffee filter (or one layer of paper towel) into a mesh strainer. Set the strainer over a bowl large enough to hold the liquid and, without stirring or shaking the liquid, pour it through the strainer. Discard the sediment left behind. Use the reserved liquid as the recipe advises. Save or freeze what you don't use and add to other cooked sauces or soups to enrich the flavor.

PASTA
Salads

Pasta salads please cooks and diners alike because they're delicious, colorful, quick to assemble, and make good use of leftovers. Don't wait for warm weather to come before trying these recipes, though. Except for Garden Macaroni Salad, which truly is a "side dish," the following recipes are every bit as satisfying as any hot pasta dish.

Chicken With Noodles and Ginger Dressing

This is a great-tasting, not too spicy pasta. Splash a tablespoon or two each of orange juice and rice vinegar over a tossed green salad and serve alongside.

12 OUNCES SPAGHETTINI

8 OUNCES SKINLESS, BONELESS
  CHICKEN BREAST, CUT INTO THIN
  STRIPS

1/2 CUP CHICKEN BROTH

2 SCALLIONS, GREEN AND WHITE
  PARTS, THINLY SLICED

1 MEDIUM RED BELL PEPPER, SEEDED
  AND CUT INTO THIN STRIPS

4 TABLESPOONS LIGHT SOY SAUCE

2 TEASPOONS SESAME OIL

1 TO 2 GARLIC CLOVES, MINCED OR
  PRESSED

2 TO 3 TEASPOONS PEELED MINCED
  FRESH GINGER

1/4 TEASPOON CRUSHED RED PEPPER
  FLAKES

2 TEASPOONS TOASTED SESAME
  SEEDS (OPTIONAL)

SERVES 4

1. Bring 4 quarts of water to a boil in a large covered pot. Add 2 teaspoons salt, if you like. Add pasta, stir, and partially cover the pot until water returns to a boil. Immediately remove cover, stir again, and cook pasta just until al dente. Drain the water from the pasta. Plunge pasta into cool water to stop the cooking. Drain again.

2. While pasta cooks, combine chicken and broth in a medium skillet. Heat to a boil over medium-high heat. Reduce heat and cover. Simmer chicken for 3 minutes, or until no longer pink inside. Transfer chicken to a serving bowl, add scallions and red pepper, and toss. Add pasta to chicken mixture. Lift with tongs or two forks to toss.

3. Strain broth into a small bowl. Add soy sauce, sesame oil, garlic, ginger, and pepper flakes and whisk to blend. Pour dressing over pasta and chicken and toss. Sprinkle sesame seeds over top. Serve warm or at room temperature.

A Quick Trick For Cooling Pasta

A salad spinner turns into a handy tool when you need to plunge pasta into cool water before serving. Separate the colander from the bowl and place colander in a clean, empty sink. Drain the water from the pasta, allowing the pasta to fall into the colander. Put the colander back into the bowl and fill with enough cold water to cover pasta. Lift the colander out of the bowl to drain water. Repeat, if necessary, until pasta feels cool to the touch.

Tricolored Tortellini Salad

Use regular tortellini with cheese if you can't find the tricolored version.

1. Bring 4 quarts of water to a boil in a large covered pot. Add 2 teaspoons salt, if you like. Add pasta, stir, and partially cover the pot until water returns to a boil. Immediately remove cover, stir again, and cook pasta until firm to the bite, about 6 minutes. Add broccoli and cook an additional 3 minutes. Just before draining, ladle out 1/2 cup pasta water and reserve. Drain the remaining water from the pasta and broccoli and plunge them into cool water to stop cooking. Drain again.

2. Combine reserved pasta water and ricotta cheese in a large serving bowl and stir until completely smooth. Add pasta to the sauce. Lift with tongs or two forks and toss to coat. Add the bell peppers, onion, and salt and pepper to taste. Toss again. Serve at room temperature.

16 OUNCES TRICOLORED TORTELLINI WITH CHEESE

2 CUPS SMALL BROCCOLI FLORETS

1 1/3 CUP DELI-STYLE SKIM RICOTTA CHEESE

1 EACH MEDIUM RED AND YELLOW BELL PEPPER, SEEDED AND CUT INTO 1-INCH SQUARES

1/2 CUP THINLY SLICED RED ONION

SALT AND FRESHLY GROUND BLACK PEPPER, TO TASTE

SERVES 6 TO 8

Dressed to Kill

Believe it or not, "cold" pasta salad actually tastes best served at room temperature, dressed just before serving. Prematurely dressed pasta often absorbs too much dressing and quickly progresses into a sticky, tasteless ball. If necessary, cook, drain, and cool pasta up to several hours before serving. You don't need to refrigerate the pasta. Simply toss pasta with a teaspoon or two of olive oil to prevent sticking. Place the pasta in a suitable serving bowl and seal tightly with plastic. Prepare other pasta salad ingredients, such as chicken, fish, or vegetables in advance, too. Refrigerate them separately, removing 30 minutes before needed. When ready to serve, add all ingredients to the pasta bowl and toss with the dressing. Serve immediately. When you absolutely have no alternative, combine pasta with additional ingredients but not dressing up to 24 hours in advance. Seal tightly and refrigerate. Remove at least 30 minutes before serving. Toss pasta salad with dressing at the last moment.

Greek-style Pasta Salad

DRESSING

1/4 CUP OLIVE OIL

1 TABLESPOON PLUS 2 TEASPOONS RED
    WINE VINEGAR

2 TABLESPOONS CHOPPED FRESH
    PARSLEY

1/2 TEASPOON DRIED OREGANO

SALT AND FRESHLY GOUND BLACK
    PEPPER, TO TASTE

SALAD

3 CUPS PENNE, SHELLS, OR ROTELLE

2 CELERY STALKS, TRIMMED AND
    SLICED

1 LARGE GREEN BELL PEPPER, STEM
    AND SEEDS REMOVED, CUT INTO
    1/2-INCH SQUARES

1 MEDIUM CUCUMBER, PEELED,
    HALVED, SEEDED, AND THINLY
    SLICED

12 CHERRY TOMATOES, STEMMED AND
    HALVED

1/2 CUP DICED RED ONION

1/4 CUP PITTED AND CHOPPED
    BRINE-CURED BLACK OLIVES

2 OUNCES FETA CHEESE, CRUMBLED

10 TO 12 LARGE LETTUCE LEAVES

SERVES 4 TO 6

When you're in the mood for something different, substitute cheese-stuffed tortellini.

1. Combine oil, vinegar, parsley, oregano, and salt and pepper to taste in a small jar with a tight-fitting lid. Cover and shake vigorously to combine.

2. Bring 4 quarts of water to a boil in a large covered pot. Add 2 teaspoons salt, if you like. Add pasta, stir, and partially cover the pot until water returns to a boil. Immediately remove cover, stir again, and cook pasta just until al dente. Drain the water from the pasta. Plunge pasta into cool water to stop the cooking. Drain again.

3. In a large serving bowl, combine celery, pepper, cucumber, tomatoes, onion, and black olives. Add pasta. Lift with tongs or two forks and toss to mix. Pour dressing over pasta salad and toss to coat. Crumble feta cheese over top. Arrange lettuce leaves around inside edge of serving bowl.

4. To serve, remove 1 or 2 leaves and place on salad plate, then heap salad on top.

It's the Pits!

Here's an easy way to pit olives. First place 2 or 3 olives side by side on a cutting board. Put the flat side of a broad knife on top of the olives and firmly press your palm on the knife to crack open each olive. Repeat with remaining olives. Pull out the pits with your fingertips.

Pasta Salad with Broccoli and Mustard Vinaigrette

The broccoli benefits from two to three hours in the mustardy marinade, but will taste terrific even with less "soaking" time.

1. Whisk together mustard, 1/4 cup water, lemon juice, and garlic in a small bowl. Slowly drizzle in olive oil, whisking constantly until thickened.

2. In a covered saucepan, steam broccoli florets over a few inches of boiling water until barely tender, 3 to 4 minutes. Plunge into a bowl of cool water to stop cooking. Drain well and pat dry with paper towels. Combine florets with raw diced broccoli stems, bell pepper, and dressing in a large bowl. Toss to coat evenly and marinate in refrigerator for at least 1 hour, or up to 4.

3. When ready to serve, bring marinated vegetables to room temperature. Bring 4 quarts of water to a boil in a large covered pot. Add 2 teaspoons salt, if you like. Add pasta, stir, and partially cover the pot until water returns to a boil. Immediately remove cover, stir again, and cook pasta just until al dente. Drain the water from the pasta. Plunge pasta into cool water to stop the cooking. Drain again.

4. Add pasta to marinated vegetables. Add Parmesan cheese, salt, and freshly ground black pepper to taste. Lift with tongs or two forks and toss to combine. Serve immediately.

DRESSING

2 TABLESPOONS DIJON OR GRAINY MUSTARD

3 TABLESPOONS FRESH LEMON JUICE

2 GARLIC CLOVES, MINCED OR PRESSED

1/3 CUP OLIVE OIL

SALAD

3 CUPS BROCCOLI FLORETS

1 CUP PEELED AND DICED BROCCOLI STEMS

1 RED BELL PEPPER, FINELY DICED

8 OUNCES PENNE OR ROTINI

3 TABLESPOONS FINELY GRATED PARMESAN CHEESE

1/4 TEASPOON SALT

FRESHLY GROUND BLACK PEPPER, TO TASTE

SERVES 4

61

Pasta Salad With Radicchio and Tuna

This recipe is especially easy to prepare and looks pretty, too. Substitute 2 cups shredded red cabbage for the radicchio if you like.

8 OUNCES PENNE OR ROTINI

1 SMALL HEAD RADICCHIO, TORN
    INTO BITE-SIZE PIECES

1/3 CUP CHOPPED SCALLIONS,
    WHITE PART ONLY

1/4 CUP MINCED FRESH PARSLEY

2 TABLESPOONS EXTRA-VIRGIN OLIVE
    OIL

JUICE OF 1 LEMON

1 CAN (6 1/2 OUNCE) SOLID WHITE
    TUNA, PACKED IN WATER, DRAINED

FRESHLY GROUND BLACK PEPPER AND
    SALT, TO TASTE

SERVES 4

1. Bring 4 quarts of water to a boil in a large covered pot. Add 2 teaspoons salt, if you like. Add pasta, stir, and partially cover the pot until water returns to a boil. Immediately remove cover, stir again, and cook pasta just until al dente. Drain the water from the pasta. Plunge pasta into cool water to stop the cooking. Drain again.

2. While pasta cooks, combine radicchio, scallions, and parsley in a large serving bowl. Add pasta, olive oil, and lemon juice. Lift with tongs or two forks and toss to coat.

3. In a small bowl, flake the tuna with a fork. Season with salt and pepper to taste. Add tuna to pasta mixture. Lift with tongs or two forks and toss gently. Season with salt, to taste. Serve at room temperature.

Buckwheat Noodles with Peppers and Sprouts

Buckwheat noodles are sold in Asian food stores, specialty shops, and large supermarkets.

1. In a small jar with tight-fitting lid, combine oil, vinegar, orange juice, ginger, garlic, and sesame seeds. Shake until thoroughly combined. Refrigerate until needed. Shake again before serving.

2. Bring 4 quarts of water to a boil in a large covered pot. Add the buckwheat noodles, stir, and bring water to a simmer. Cover the pot and simmer until noodles are almost tender, about 5 minutes. Drain water from the noodles. Plunge noodles into cool water to stop the cooking. Drain again.

3. In a large serving bowl, mix together tomatoes, red pepper, yellow pepper, bean sprouts, cilantro, and cooled noodles. Pour the dressing over ingredients and toss to coat. Serve at room temperature.

DRESSING

3 TABLESPOONS CANOLA OIL

3 TABLESPOONS RICE WINE VINEGAR

2 TABLESPOONS ORANGE JUICE OR
WATER

1/2 TEASPOON CHOPPED FRESH
GINGER

1 GARLIC CLOVE, MINCED OR PRESSED

2 TEASPOONS TOASTED SESAME SEEDS

SALAD

12 OUNCES BUCKWHEAT NOODLES

2 LARGE RIPE TOMATOES, CUT INTO
1/2-INCH CUBES

1 MEDIUM RED BELL PEPPER, CUT INTO
JULIENNE STRIPS

1 MEDIUM YELLOW BELL PEPPER, CUT
INTO JULIENNE STRIPS

1/2 CUP FRESH BEAN SPROUTS

1/4 CUP FINELY CHOPPED FRESH
CILANTRO OR PARSLEY

SERVES 4

How to Toast Seeds and Nuts

Toasted seeds and nuts add crunch and flavor, and gracefully garnish many dishes. To toast, stir and toss seeds or nuts in a dry pan over medium-low heat until they turn an even golden brown. Remove from the pan immediately, as the nuts will continue to darken off the heat.

Pasta Salad With Fresh Tomato and Basil

3 MEDIUM-SIZE RIPE TOMATOES, CUT
    INTO 1/4-INCH DICE
1 TABLESPOON EXTRA-VIRGIN OLIVE
    OIL
1 TABLESPOON BALSAMIC OR RED
    WINE VINEGAR
3 LARGE GARLIC CLOVES, MINCED OR
    PRESSED
1/2 CUP LOOSELY PACKED FRESH
    BASIL LEAVES, TORN INTO STRIPS
2 TABLESPOONS CHOPPED FRESH
    PARSLEY
SALT AND FRESHLY GROUND PEPPER,
    TO TASTE
12 OUNCES VERMICELLI OR
    SPAGHETTINI
2 OUNCES FETA CHEESE

SERVES 4

1. In a large serving bowl, gently toss together tomatoes, oil, vinegar, garlic, basil, parsley, and salt and pepper to taste.

2. Bring 4 quarts of water to a boil in a large covered pot. Add 2 teaspoons salt, if you like. Add pasta, stir, and partially cover the pot until water returns to a boil. Immediately remove cover, stir again, and cook pasta just until al dente. Drain water from pasta.

3. Add pasta to salad. Lift with tongs or two forks and toss. Crumble feta cheese over the top. Serve immediately.

It's So Easy Being Green

Pale-looking, overcooked greens such as snow peas, green beans, and broccoli are a sorry sight in pasta salad. To keep your greens "green," drain and immerse them briefly in cold water immediately after cooking. This stops the cooking process and sets their color. Drain the vegetables well and pat dry with paper towels before adding to the salad.

Tabbooleh-style Couscous Salad

Quick-cooking whole-wheat couscous has a delicious nutty taste.

1. Bring 1 1/4 cups water to a boil in a medium covered pot, then stir in couscous. Reduce heat and simmer, covered, for 5 minutes. Remove from heat, but don't remove cover until all water is absorbed, about 5 more minutes.

2. Transfer couscous to a medium serving bowl and cool for 10 minutes. Toss lightly with a fork. Add parsley, tomatoes, scallions, chick-peas, and mint. Toss together.

3. Combine oil, lemon juice, and salt in a small jar with a tight-fitting lid. Shake vigorously to combine. Pour dressing over couscous mixture and toss to combine. Cover and refrigerate for 1 to 2 hours to allow flavors to blend. Serve at room temperature.

1 CUP QUICK-COOKING WHOLE- WHEAT COUSCOUS

2 CUPS MINCED FRESH PARSLEY

2 MEDIUM-SIZE RIPE TOMATOES, SEEDED AND CUT INTO 1/4-INCH DICE

4 SCALLIONS, WHITE AND GREEN PARTS, MINCED

1/2 CUP COOKED CHICK-PEAS, RINSED AND DRAINED IF CANNED

2 TABLESPOONS MINCED FRESH MINT LEAVES

1/4 CUP OLIVE OIL

1/4 CUP FRESH LEMON JUICE

SALT, TO TASTE

SERVES 4

Smart Shopping

Most supermarkets carry packages of couscous that contain their own flavor packet. While these brands taste good, buying plain couscous in the amount you want *in bulk* from the health food store saves you a small bundle of money. Use 1 1/2 cups water for each cup of couscous. Season the cooking liquid with your own spices, then cover and bring to a boil. Add the couscous and remove from heat. Cover and let stand for 5 minutes. Toss lightly with a fork before serving. You could also add some cooked beans, peas, or corn when you add the couscous. Spice combinations might include minced fresh herbs, ginger and garlic, or curry, cumin, and cinnamon.

Garden Macaroni Salad

Serve this lighter version of an old-time favorite with sandwiches made from freshly cooked and sliced store-bought turkey.

8 OUNCES ELBOW MACARONI
1/2 CUP LIGHT MAYONNAISE
1/2 CUP PLAIN LOW-FAT YOGURT
2 TABLESPOONS WHITE VINEGAR
1/2 TEASPOON SALT
FRESHLY GROUND BLACK PEPPER,
    TO TASTE
2 CELERY STALKS, DICED
1 LARGE RED OR GREEN BELL PEPPER,
    SEEDED AND DICED
1 LARGE CARROT, PEELED AND DICED

SERVES 6

1. Bring 4 quarts of water to a boil in a large covered pot. Add 2 teaspoons salt, if you like. Add pasta, stir, and partially cover the pot until water returns to a boil. Immediately remove cover, stir again, and cook pasta just until al dente. Drain water from the pasta. Plunge pasta into cool water to stop the cooking. Drain again.

2. In a large serving bowl, stir together mayonnaise, yogurt, vinegar, salt, and pepper to taste. Add macaroni, celery, pepper, and carrot. Lift with tongs or two forks and toss to coat. Cover and refrigerate until ready to serve.

Fresh Tomato Pasta Salad

Use whatever fresh, flavorful tomatoes you have on hand. Serve with grilled bread.

1. Bring 4 quarts of water to a boil in a large covered pot. Add 2 teaspoons salt, if you like. Add pasta, stir, and partially cover the pot until water returns to a boil. Immediately remove cover, stir again, and cook pasta just until al dente. Drain water from the pasta. Plunge pasta into cool water to stop the cooking. Drain again.

2. While pasta cooks, purée olives and olive oil in a food processor or blender. Stir in lemon juice and Cognac. Set aside.

3. In a large serving bowl, combine pasta with olive mixture. Lift with tongs or two forks and toss to coat. Add tomatoes, capers, red onion, parsley, and salt and pepper to taste. Toss gently. Serve at room temperature.

12 OUNCES PENNE

1/2 CUP PITTED, BRINE-PACKED BLACK OLIVES

3 TABLESPOONS EXTRA-VIRGIN OLIVE OIL

1 TABLESPOON FRESH LEMON JUICE

1 TEASPOON COGNAC (OPTIONAL)

1 POUND RIPE TOMATOES, CUT INTO BITE-SIZE CHUNKS

1 TABLESPOON CAPERS, RINSED AND DRAINED

1/4 CUP SLIVERED RED ONION

2 TABLESPOONS MINCED FRESH PARSLEY

SALT AND FRESHLY GROUND BLACK PEPPER, TO TASTE

SERVES 4 TO 6

Mediterranean-style Pasta Salad with Citrus Vinaigrette

Orange juice, not oil, predominates in this flavorful pasta salad.

VINAIGRETTE

1/3 CUP OLIVE OIL

1/3 CUP FRESH ORANGE JUICE

2 TO 3 GARLIC CLOVES, MINCED OR
    PRESSED

3 TABLESPOONS VINEGAR OR LEMON
    JUICE

1/2 TEASPOON DRIED OREGANO, OR
    1 TABLESPOON MINCED FRESH
    HERBS, SUCH AS MINT OR PARSLEY

SALT AND FRESHLY GROUND BLACK
    PEPPER, TO TASTE

SALAD

8 OUNCES RADIATORE, FUSILLI, OR
    PENNE

1 CAN (12 1/2 OUNCES) SOLID WHITE
    TUNA, PACKED IN WATER, DRAINED

1/2 JAR (7 OUNCES) ROASTED RED
    PEPPERS, RINSED, WELL DRAINED,
    AND CUT INTO THIN STRIPS

6 BRINE-CURED BLACK OLIVES,
    PITTED AND HALVED

1/2 CUP DICED RED ONION

1/2 CUP DICED CELERY

3 TABLESPOONS CHOPPED FRESH
    PARSLEY

4 TO 8 LARGE LETTUCE LEAVES FOR
    GARNISH

SERVES 4

1. Combine olive oil, orange juice, garlic, vinegar, and oregano in a small jar with a tight-fitting lid. Shake vigorously, then season to taste with salt and pepper. Set aside.

2. Bring 4 quarts of water to a boil in a large covered pot. Add 2 teaspoons salt, if you like. Add the pasta, stir, and partially cover the pot until water returns to a boil. Immediately remove cover, stir again, and cook pasta just until al dente. Drain water from the pasta. Plunge pasta into cool water to stop the cooking. Drain well.

3. In a medium serving bowl, flake the tuna, then add the roasted peppers, olives, onion, celery, parsley, and cooled pasta. Toss together gently. Shake vinaigrette before pouring over the salad, then lift with tongs or two forks and toss gently to coat. Serve on a bed of lettuce.

Have You Herb?

Tough-leaved herbs, such as thyme, oregano, and rosemary, may taste more flavorful dried than fresh. The reason? During the drying process, cellular breakdown allows for the extraction of more oil, making a more potent herb. Cooking with good-quality dried herbs, instead of fresh, may be a better choice.

Fresh, tough-leaved herbs can benefit from brief cooking prior to use. Combine 1 to 2 teaspoons olive oil with 1 to 2 tablespoons of the fresh herb in a small skillet. Cook over low heat just until aroma is released, then use as recipe advises.

Soft-leaved herbs, such as basil, parsley, and cilantro, *lose* most of their distinctive flavor during the drying process. For the best flavor, you should use these herbs in their fresh form only.

Learn to rely on your own judgment. If you like, follow the recipe's suggestion to use fresh herbs, then substitute dry herbs the next time around to determine which tastes better. To substitute dry herbs for fresh, use about one third of the amount suggested for fresh herbs.

Buckwheat Noodles with Veggies and Scallion Vinaigrette

Buckwheat noodles cook in minutes. Make the vinaigrette and vegetables up to 24 hours in advance and store separately, covered, in the refrigerator. Remove 30 minutes before serving.

VINAIGRETTE

1/4 CUP THINLY SLICED SCALLIONS, WHITE PART ONLY

3 TABLESPOONS RICE VINEGAR

1 TEASPOON HONEY

1/3 CUP ORANGE JUICE

2 TABLESPOONS CANOLA OIL

SALT AND FRESHLY GROUND BLACK PEPPER, TO TASTE

SALAD

8 OUNCES BUCKWHEAT NOODLES

2 CARROTS, TRIMMED, PEELED, AND CUT ON DIAGONAL INTO THIN SLICES

1/2 POUND GREEN BEANS, CUT ON DIAGONAL INTO 1/2-INCH PIECES

1 CUP MUNG BEANS

1/4 CUP THINLY SLICED SCALLIONS, WHITE PART ONLY

SERVES 4

1. Purée scallions, rice vinegar, and honey in a food processor or blender. Add orange juice and oil and process until well blended. Season to taste with salt and pepper. Set vinaigrette aside.

2. Bring 4 quarts of water to a boil in a large covered pot. Add the noodles, stir, and bring water to a simmer. Cover the pot and simmer until noodles are almost tender, about 5 minutes. Just before draining, ladle out 2 cups cooking water and reserve. Drain the remaining water from the noodles. Plunge noodles into cool water to stop the cooking. Drain again. Transfer to a serving bowl.

3. Using the same pot, bring reserved water to a boil. Add carrots and green beans; cover, and cook for 2 to 3 minutes, until vegetables are crisp-tender. Drain and plunge into a bowl of cool water. When completely cool, drain again.

4. Add carrots, green beans, mung beans, and scallions to noodles. Lift with tongs or two forks and toss. Pour vinaigrette over salad and toss to coat.

Green Bean Pointer

Save time preparing green beans—don't bother trimming any short, thin tips before cooking. To trim thicker tips, hold a handful of beans, exposing tips above your fist. Snip off with kitchen scissors, then repeat at other end.

Italian

Classics

These are some of my favorite recipes. They cook quickly, taste delicious, and require nothing more than a thick slice of crusty bread and a simple dessert to complete the meal.

While the term "classics" often conjures up specific pasta dishes, you won't find a definitive recipe for any one of them. Each region in Italy has its own version of the same recipe, and all are authentic.

With a wink toward the traditional, these reduced-fat sauces retain their delicious flavor. What a wonderful hand-me-down to those you love.

Bolognese Sauce

You won't miss the taste of beef in this flavorful, lower-fat version of classic bolognese sauce.

1 TABLESPOON OLIVE OIL

1/3 CUP EACH FINELY CHOPPED
    ONION, CARROT, AND CELERY

1 1/2 POUNDS GROUND TURKEY

SALT AND FRESHLY GROUND BLACK
    PEPPER, TO TASTE

1/2 CUP DRY WHITE WINE OR
    CHICKEN BROTH

1/3 CUP LOW-FAT MILK

1/8 TEASPOON FRESHLY GRATED
    NUTMEG

1 CAN (28 OUNCE) ITALIAN-STYLE PLUM
    TOMATOES, UNDRAINED

FRESHLY GRATED PARMESAN CHEESE

MAKES ABOUT 1 QUART, ENOUGH
FOR 16 OUNCES PASTA

1. Heat oil in a 4- to 5-quart saucepan over medium-high heat. Add the onion, carrot, and celery and cook, stirring, until onion is soft, about 3 minutes.

2. Crumble the ground turkey into the pan and season with salt and pepper to taste. Cook, stirring occasionally, until turkey loses its pink color, but barely browns. Add wine and cook over high heat, stirring occasionally, until wine completely evaporates. Add milk, stirring, until most of the milk has evaporated, about 2 minutes.

3. Add nutmeg and undrained tomatoes. With the back of a wooden spoon, break up tomatoes against side of pot until small pieces are formed. Bring sauce to a boil. Reduce heat to low and simmer uncovered, stirring occasionally, for 1 hour. Adjust seasonings. Use immediately or allow to cool to room temperature. Refrigerate in a closed container for up to 2 days, or freeze for up to 6 months. Toss with hot pasta and cheese.

Marinara Sauce

Fresh tomato sauce is a staple around my house. This recipe makes more than enough for 4 servings, and I freeze what we don't eat for later use. If you prefer, halve the recipe.

Heat oil in a heavy 3- to 4-quart saucepan over medium heat. Add onion and garlic and cook, stirring, for 2 minutes. Add tomato paste and reserved juice from canned tomatoes. Cook and stir constantly for 2 minutes longer. Add tomatoes, oregano, basil, and sugar. Break up tomatoes with the back of a spoon as you stir sauce. Cook, stirring occasionally, until sauce comes to a gentle simmer. Reduce heat and continue to simmer, uncovered, for about 1 hour. Season to taste with salt and pepper. Just before serving, stir parsley into sauce.

2 TABLESPOONS OLIVE OIL

1/2 CUP MINCED ONION

2 GARLIC CLOVES, MINCED OR PRESSED

1 TABLESPOON TOMATO PASTE

2 CANS (28 OUNCES EACH) ITALIAN-STYLE PLUM TOMATOES, JUICES OF ONE RESERVED

2 TEASPOONS DRIED OREGANO

2 TEASPOONS DRIED BASIL

1/2 TEASPOON SUGAR (OPTIONAL)

SALT AND FRESHLY GROUND BLACK PEPPER, TO TASTE

1/4 CUP PACKED MINCED FRESH PARSLEY

MAKES ABOUT **6 CUPS**, ENOUGH FOR **2 POUNDS** PASTA

Pasta Prejudice

Freshly made pasta tastes superb, and I salute you if you make your own. Packaged fresh pasta tastes great, too, but forget any preconceived notions about dried pasta not being up to snuff. High-quality, imported dried pasta produces an equally delicious dish. Fresh pasta does cook quicker than dried, but remember—although priced slightly higher than domestically dried pasta—imported dried pasta remains far less expensive than fresh.

Pasta Primavera

Fresh produce and a quickly made sauce make pasta primavera a springtime favorite. Substitute 1 small onion, diced, if you don't have leeks.

12 OUNCES BOW TIES
2 TABLESPOONS OLIVE OIL
1/4 CUP FINELY CHOPPED LEEKS,
    WHITE PART ONLY
1/2 CUP FINELY DICED CARROTS
2/3 CUP FINELY DICED YELLOW OR
    GREEN SUMMER SQUASH
3/4 CUP DICED RED BELL PEPPER
1/4 CUP DRY WHITE WINE
1 CUP CHICKEN BROTH
16 ASPARAGUS SPEARS, TOUGH ENDS
    SNAPPED OFF, SPEARS SLICED INTO
    1/2-INCH LENGTHS
1/4 CUP MINCED FRESH BASIL, OR
    DILL LEAVES
FRESHLY GRATED PARMESAN CHEESE

SERVES 4

1. Bring 4 quarts of water to a boil in a large covered pot. Add pasta, stir, and partially cover the pot until water returns to a boil. Immediately remove cover, stir again, and cook pasta just until al dente. Drain water from pasta and return to covered pot, off the heat, if sauce is not ready.

2. While pasta cooks, heat oil in a nonstick skillet over medium-high heat. Add leeks and carrots and cook, stirring frequently, until leeks are limp, about 5 minutes. Add squash and red pepper and cook for 3 minutes longer. Add white wine, cover, and simmer over low heat until vegetables start to soften, about 3 minutes. Add the chicken broth and bring to a simmer over medium heat. Add asparagus, cover, and simmer over medium heat until asparagus is barely cooked, 3 to 4 minutes.

3. Add sauce and basil to pasta. Lift with tongs or two forks and toss until well mixed. Serve immediately, with Parmesan cheese.

Basil Hint

Just prior to chopping, pour one or two drops of olive oil on fresh basil leaves to prevent them from turning black.

Tagliatelle with Nutmeg and Peas

This recipe cooks in no time. It is a close cousin to the classic Alfredo sauce, which is made with heavy cream and butter.

1. Bring 4 quarts of water to a boil in a large covered pot. Add 2 teaspoons salt, if you like. Add pasta, stir, and partially cover the pot until water returns to a boil. Immediately remove cover, stir again, and cook pasta just until al dente, adding peas for final 2 minutes of cooking. Drain water from pasta and peas and return to covered pot, off the heat.

2. While pasta cooks, heat milk, half-and-half, and nutmeg in a small saucepan, just until tiny bubbles appear around edge of the pan. Do not boil.

3. Add sauce and cheese to the pasta and peas. Over low heat, lift with tongs or two forks and toss to coat, for about 1 minute. Season to taste with salt and pepper. Serve immediately.

12 OUNCES TAGLIATELLE OR FETTUCCINE
1 CUP FRESH OR FROZEN PEAS
1 1/4 CUPS LOW-FAT MILK
1/4 CUP HALF-AND-HALF OR LIGHT CREAM
2 PINCHES OF FRESHLY GRATED NUTMEG
1/4 CUP FRESHLY GRATED PARMESAN CHEESE
SALT AND FRESHLY GROUND BLACK PEPPER, TO TASTE

SERVES 4

Penne Rigati With Vodka Tomato Cream Sauce

This classic sauce surfaced in the '80s—the 1980s, that is—and is still going strong! Serve this dish alone or accompanied by a simply broiled or steamed fish.

12 OUNCES PENNE RIGATI

2 TABLESPOONS EXTRA-VIRGIN OLIVE
    OIL

1/4 TEASPOON CRUSHED RED PEPPER
    FLAKES, OR MORE TO TASTE

1/4 CUP VODKA

2 CUPS CANNED ITALIAN-STYLE PLUM
    TOMATOES, DRAINED AND PURÉED

1/4 CUP HEAVY CREAM

SALT AND FRESHLY GROUND BLACK
    PEPPER, TO TASTE

FRESHLY GRATED PARMESAN CHEESE

SERVES 4

1. Bring 4 quarts of water to a boil in a large covered pot. Add 2 teaspoons salt, if you like. Add pasta, stir, and partially cover the pot until water returns to a boil. Immediately remove cover, stir again, and cook pasta just until al dente. Drain water from pasta and return to covered pot, off the heat, if sauce is not ready.

2. While pasta cooks, heat oil and crushed red pepper flakes in a medium skillet over low heat for 2 minutes, or just until fragrant. Add vodka all at once, stirring over medium-high heat, and simmer for 2 minutes. Stir in puréed tomatoes, cream, salt and pepper to taste. Cook until heated through, 3 to 4 minutes, stirring occasionally. *Do not allow mixture to boil.*

3. Add pasta to sauce. Over low heat, lift with tongs or two forks and toss to coat for about 1 minute. Serve with Parmesan cheese.

Straw and Hay

This classic combination of two Italian favorites, green and plain fettuccine, is sauced with chicken broth and a small amount of cream.

1. Bring 4 quarts of water to a boil in a large covered pot. Add 2 teaspoons salt, if you like. Add pasta, stir, and partially cover the pot until water returns to a boil. Immediately remove cover, stir again, and cook pasta just until al dente. Drain water from pasta and return to covered pot, off the heat.

2. While pasta cooks, combine heavy cream and chicken broth in a large skillet over medium heat and bring to a boil. Add ham and peas, reduce heat to low, and simmer, uncovered, for 3 minutes. Remove from heat.

3. Add pasta to sauce. Over low heat, lift with tongs or two forks and toss lightly for 2 to 3 minutes, until pasta absorbs most of the liquid. Serve with Parmesan cheese.

4 OUNCES PLAIN FETTUCCINE

4 OUNCES GREEN FETTUCCINE

1/4 CUP HEAVY CREAM

3/4 CUP CHICKEN BROTH OR CANNED LOW-SODIUM BROTH

1/2 CUP JULIENNE STRIPS OF THINLY SLICED COOKED HAM

1/3 CUP FROZEN TINY PEAS

FRESHLY GRATED PARMESAN CHEESE

SERVES 4

Puttanesca

This is a very simple recipe that you make out of the pantry.

1 TABLESPOON OLIVE OIL

1 TIN (2 OUNCES) ANCHOVY
    FILLETS, RINSED AND DRAINED

1 TEASPOON MINCED OR PRESSED
    GARLIC

1 CAN (28 OUNCES) ITALIAN-STYLE
    PEELED TOMATOES, CHOPPED,
    JUICES RESERVED

1 CUP CHOPPED FRESH PARSLEY

1 TEASPOON DRIED OREGANO

1/4 TEASPOON CRUSHED RED PEPPER
    FLAKES, OR TO TASTE

1/3 CUP PITTED AND SLICED BRINE-
    CURED BLACK OLIVES

1 TABLESPOON CAPERS, RINSED AND
    DRAINED

12 OUNCES SPAGHETTI OR LINGUINE

SERVES 4

1. Heat oil in a large nonstick skillet over medium heat. Add anchovies and mash to a paste with a wooden spoon. Add garlic and cook, stirring, for 1 minute. Add tomatoes, reserved juices, parsley, oregano, and red pepper flakes and bring to a boil. Reduce the heat, cover, and simmer until sauce is slightly thickened, stirring occasionally, about 20 minutes. Stir in olives and capers.

2. While sauce simmers, bring 4 quarts of water to a boil in a large covered pot. Add 2 teaspoons salt, if you like. Add pasta, stir, and partially cover the pot until water returns to a boil. Immediately remove cover, stir again, and cook pasta just until al dente. Drain water from pasta and return to covered pot, off the heat, if sauce is not ready.

3. Add pasta to sauce. Over low heat, lift with tongs or two forks and toss until pasta is heated through, about 2 minutes. Serve immediately.

Spaghettini with Garlic and Olive Oil

The easiest of pastas to prepare is one of the most delicious, too.

1. Bring 4 quarts of water to a boil in a large covered pot. Add 2 teaspoons salt, if you like. Add pasta, stir, and partially cover the pot until water returns to a boil. Immediately remove cover, stir again, and cook pasta just until al dente. Drain water from pasta and return to covered pot, off the heat, if sauce is not ready. Add chicken broth and toss to coat.

2. While pasta cooks, warm the oil and garlic in a large skillet over medium-high heat, stirring constantly until garlic begins to release its aroma, about 30 seconds. Remove skillet from heat. Stir in parsley, red pepper flakes, and salt.

3. Add pasta to sauce. Over low heat, lift with tongs or two forks and toss to coat for 1 minute. Serve immediately.

12 OUNCES SPAGHETTINI

1/4 CUP CHICKEN BROTH

2 TABLESPOONS EXTRA-VIRGIN OLIVE OIL

2 TO 3 LARGE GARLIC CLOVES, MINCED OR PRESSED

1 TABLESPOON MINCED PARSLEY

1/4 TEASPOON CRUSHED RED PEPPER FLAKES

1/4 TEASPOON SALT

SERVES 4 TO 6

Penne All'Arrabbiata

This sauce is hot, hot, hot! Cut back on the dried red pepper to curb the heat.

12 OUNCES PENNE

3 TABLESPOONS EXTRA-VIRGIN OLIVE
OIL

1/2 TEASPOON CRUSHED RED PEPPER
FLAKES, OR TO TASTE

2 GARLIC CLOVES, MINCED OR PRESSED

1 CAN (28 OUNCES) PEELED ITALIAN-
STYLE PLUM TOMATOES WITH
JUICES, PURÉED IN FOOD
PROCESSOR OR BLENDER

SALT, TO TASTE

1/4 CUP FINELY CHOPPED FRESH
PARSLEY

SERVES 4

1. Bring 4 quarts of water to a boil in a large covered pot. Add 2 teaspoons salt, if you like. Add pasta, stir, and partially cover the pot until water returns to a boil. Immediately remove cover, stir again, and cook pasta just until al dente. Drain water from pasta and return to covered pot, off the heat.

2. Meanwhile, heat oil in a medium skillet over low heat. Add red pepper flakes and cook for 1 to 2 minutes, until oil begins to color slightly. Add garlic and cook 15 seconds longer. Add puréed tomatoes and simmer sauce, uncovered, stirring often, until sauce thickens and reduces slightly, about 20 minutes. Remove from heat and add salt to taste.

3. Add sauce and chopped parsley to the pasta. Over low heat, lift with tongs or two forks and toss to coat for 1 minute. Serve immediately.

PASTA
Without Meat

Pasta without meat is not just a first course or side dish anymore. When cooked with a variety of vegetables, beans, and spices, meatless pasta dishes are healthy and easy to prepare, and they're filling too. For all of us who are determined to direct our taste buds toward healthier foods, pasta without meat leads us to great choices.

Mad About Mushrooms and Pasta

I love the taste of mushrooms, and this simple, uncomplicated pasta overflows with them.

1 PACKAGE (ABOUT 1 OUNCE) DRIED
    PORCINI MUSHROOMS
12 OUNCES PERCIATELLI OR
    SPAGHETTI
1/4 CUP CHOPPED SHALLOTS
1 TABLESPOON OLIVE OIL
1 BOX (10 OUNCES) FRESH WHITE
    BUTTON MUSHROOMS, WIPED CLEAN
    AND THINLY SLICED
1 TEASPOON DRIED CHERVIL
SALT AND FRESHLY GROUND BLACK
    PEPPER, TO TASTE
1 TABLESPOON FLOUR
1 CUP DRY WHITE WINE, OR BROTH
FRESHLY GRATED PARMESAN CHEESE

SERVES 4 TO 6

1. In a small saucepan, bring 1 1/4 cups water to a boil. Add porcini mushrooms. Bring to a boil, cover, remove from heat, and let soak for 20 minutes. Use a slotted spoon to remove mushrooms. Reserve soaking liquid. Rinse mushrooms in fresh water to remove any grit, then squeeze dry. Place a paper towel in a small mesh strainer and set over a clean bowl. Pour soaking liquid through strainer. Set mushrooms and strained soaking liquid aside.

2. Bring 4 quarts of water to a boil in a large covered pot. Add 2 teaspoons salt, if you like. Add pasta, stir, and partially cover the pot until water returns to a boil. Immediately remove cover, stir again, and cook pasta just until al dente. Drain water from pasta and return to covered pot, off the heat, if sauce is not ready.

3. While pasta cooks, heat shallots and olive oil in a large non-stick skillet over medium heat. Cook, stirring often, until shallots soften, 4 to 5 minutes. Add button mushrooms, chervil, and salt and pepper. Cook, stirring often, for 6 to 8 minutes, until mushrooms begin to soften. Add soaked porcini mushrooms, flour, wine, and strained soaking liquid. Simmer on medium-high heat, stirring constantly, for 3 to 4 minutes, just until sauce thickens.

4. To serve, divide pasta among 4 warmed bowls and spoon sauce over top. Sprinkle with Parmesan cheese. Serve at once.

Stove-Top Macaroni and Cheese

This recipe makes a delicious lower-fat alternative to traditional macaroni and cheese.

1. Bring 4 quarts of water to a boil in a large covered pot. Add 2 teaspoons salt, if you like. Add pasta, stir, and partially cover the pot until water returns to a boil. Immediately remove cover, stir again, and cook pasta just until al dente. Drain water from pasta and return to covered pot, off the heat.

2. While pasta cooks, combine cottage cheese and 1/2 cup milk in a food processor or blender and spin until smooth.

3. Combine flour and remaining 1 1/4 cups milk in a medium saucepan and whisk together until smooth. Cook the mixture over medium-high heat, stirring constantly, until it comes to a boil. Reduce heat and simmer for 3 minutes, stirring often, until thickened. Add cottage cheese mixture, Cheddar cheese, and nutmeg. Cook over low heat for 3 to 4 minutes, stirring often, until sauce is hot and smooth. Cover and remove from heat.

4. Pour sauce over pasta and mix gently but thoroughly. Season with salt and white pepper to taste. Cover and cook over low heat for 4 to 6 minutes, stirring occasionally, until sauce is thick and bubbly. Transfer to a serving bowl and sprinkle with parsley, if you like. Serve immediately.

3 CUPS ELBOW MACARONI

1 CONTAINER (16 OUNCES) LOW-FAT COTTAGE CHEESE (ABOUT 1 3/4 CUPS)

1 3/4 CUPS SKIM MILK

2 TABLESPOONS ALL-PURPOSE FLOUR

1 1/2 CUPS SHREDDED SHARP CHEDDAR CHEESE

1/4 TEASPOON FRESHLY GRATED NUTMEG

SALT AND FRESHLY GROUND WHITE PEPPER, TO TASTE

1 TABLESPOON MINCED PARSLEY (OPTIONAL)

SERVES 4

Capellini with Cherry Tomatoes, Basil, and Lemon

So quick and easy. Substitute 1/3 cup boiling pasta water for the broth, if necessary.

8 OUNCES CAPELLINI

2 TABLESPOONS UNSALTED BUTTER

1/3 CUP CHICKEN BROTH

10 CHERRY TOMATOES, CUT IN HALF

1 TABLESPOON GRATED LEMON PEEL

3 TABLESPOONS FRESH LEMON JUICE

1/4 CUP SHREDDED FRESH BASIL
   LEAVES

SALT AND FRESHLY GROUND BLACK
   PEPPER, TO TASTE

FRESHLY GRATED PARMESAN CHEESE

SERVES 4

1. Bring 4 quarts of water to a boil in a large covered pot. Add 2 teaspoons salt, if you like. Add pasta, stir, and partially cover the pot until water returns to a boil. Immediately remove cover, stir again, and cook pasta just until al dente. Just before draining, ladle out 1/3 cup cooking water and reserve if substituting for broth. Drain remaining water from pasta and return to covered pot, off the heat, if sauce is not ready.

2. While pasta cooks, melt butter in a medium skillet over low heat, stirring constantly until bubbly. Quickly stir in broth, cherry tomato halves, lemon peel, and juice. Cover and heat gently for 1 minute. Remove from heat.

3. Add pasta to sauce. Over low heat, lift with tongs or two forks and toss to coat for 1 minute. Remove from heat and toss in basil leaves. Season with salt and pepper. Serve immediately with Parmesan cheese.

Penne with Spinach and Almonds

1. Bring 4 quarts of water to a boil in a large covered pot. Add 2 teaspoons salt, if you like. Add pasta, stir, and partially cover the pot until water returns to a boil. Immediately remove cover, stir again, and cook pasta just until al dente. Drain water from pasta and return to covered pot, off the heat, if sauce is not ready.

2. While pasta cooks, toast almonds in a large skillet over medium heat, stirring constantly, for 1 minute, until barely golden. Transfer almonds to a small bowl.

3. Add olive oil and garlic to skillet. Cook over medium heat, stirring constantly, for 30 seconds, until garlic turns golden. Add broth, spinach, raisins, and tomatoes. Cover and cook over medium-high heat for 3 minutes, or just until spinach wilts. Remove skillet from heat.

4. Add pasta and toasted almonds to spinach mixture. Over low heat, lift with tongs or two forks and toss to coat for 1 minute, to heat through. Transfer to a serving bowl. Serve with Parmesan cheese.

8 OUNCES PENNE

2 TABLESPOONS SLICED ALMONDS

1 TABLESPOON OLIVE OIL

1 GARLIC CLOVE, MINCED OR PRESSED

1/2 CUP CHICKEN OR VEGETABLE BROTH

1 LARGE BUNCH SPINACH, WASHED, THICK STEMS REMOVED

2 TABLESPOONS GOLDEN RAISINS

2 MEDIUM-SIZE RIPE PLUM TOMATOES, PEELED AND DICED

FRESHLY GRATED PARMESAN CHEESE

SERVES 4

FAT FREE

To reduce fat calories in your diet, try steaming onion, garlic, and spices together instead of cooking them in oil. Use approximately 1/4 cup liquid—broth, water, or even the drained juices from canned tomatoes—for every 1 cup chopped onion. To steam, pour the liquid into a skillet on medium heat and add onion, garlic, and spices. Cover and steam until soft, 2 to 3 minutes. Don't allow the liquid to evaporate entirely or the onion will stick to the pan. Add more liquid if necessary. After steaming, continue as directed in your recipe.

Butternut Squash with Penne and Lightly Browned Butter

A small amount of browned butter gives this pasta dish a burst of flavor.

12 OUNCES PENNE

1 BUTTERNUT SQUASH, 2 TO 2 1/2 POUNDS, SEEDED, PEELED, AND CUT INTO 1/2-INCH DICE (SEE NOTE)

3 TABLESPOONS BUTTER

1/8 TEASPOON FRESHLY GRATED NUTMEG

SALT AND FRESHLY GROUND BLACK PEPPER, TO TASTE

2 TABLESPOONS FRESHLY GRATED PARMESAN CHEESE

2 AMARETTI OR OTHER ANISE-FLAVORED COOKIES, CRUSHED (OPTIONAL)

SERVES 4 TO 6

1. Bring 4 quarts of water to a boil in a large covered pot. Add 2 teaspoons salt, if you like. Add pasta, stir, and partially cover the pot until water returns to a boil. Immediately remove cover, stir again, and cook pasta just until al dente. Drain water from pasta and return to covered pot, off the heat.

2. While pasta cooks, steam squash over 3 inches boiling water, until tender, 12 to 15 minutes. Remove squash and add to pasta. Recover the pot.

3. In a small heavy saucepan, melt butter over medium-low heat and allow it to boil gently. Stir constantly for 1 minute, or until foaming stops. At this point, butter should be a pale golden color, but not browned. Immediately remove pan from heat. Pour butter over pasta and squash, using a small spatula to scrape it out.

4. Over low heat, lift pasta with tongs or two forks and toss to coat for 1 minute. Add nutmeg, salt and pepper to taste, and Parmesan cheese and toss again. Place in warm serving bowl and sprinkle with amaretti cookie crumbs. Serve at once.

Note: *The flesh of butternut squash is very firm and its outer skin is somewhat tough. Use a very sharp knife to halve squash lengthwise, starting at base of the large neck. Scoop out the seeds and any fibers, then peel the squash. Cut the peeled squash crosswise into 1/2-inch-thick slices, and cut each slice into 1/2-inch dice.*

Browned Butter

The flavor and aroma of browned butter heightens the butter's flavor so you feel as if you're eating much more than a tiny bit. Use browned butter when you want to add flavor without adding too much fat. Spoon over steamed vegetables or toss with pasta, adding a little bit of freshly grated cheese.

Oven-Dried Cherry Tomatoes with Orecchiette and Ricotta Salata

You can purchase ricotta salata, a sharp sheep's milk cheese, at fine cheese counters and specialty stores. Feta cheese is a good substitute, if necessary.

1 PINT RIPE CHERRY TOMATOES

2 TABLESPOONS EXTRA-VIRGIN OLIVE OIL

12 OUNCES ORECCHIETTE

1 TO 2 GARLIC CLOVES, MINCED OR PRESSED

SALT TO TASTE

1/4 CUP GRATED PARMESAN CHEESE

1/2 CUP RICOTTA SALATA SLIVERS, SHAVED FROM A 4-OUNCE CHUNK

FRESHLY GROUND BLACK PEPPER, TO TASTE

SERVES 6

1. Early in the day or the night before serving, heat a gas oven to 300°F (an electric oven doesn't stay hot when it's turned off). Cut tomatoes in half through stem end and put them on a cake rack, cut side up. Put in preheated oven, turn off heat, and leave undisturbed for up to 12 hours. Tomatoes should look shriveled and dried on the outside and will be soft on the inside.

2. Layer tomatoes loosely in one or two jars and add olive oil. Shake a few times to douse the tomatoes with oil. Seal tightly and store in the refrigerator until ready to use.

3. Bring 4 quarts of water to a boil in a large covered pot. Add 2 teaspoons salt, if you like. Add pasta, stir, and partially cover the pot until water returns to a boil. Immediately remove cover, stir again, and cook pasta just until al dente. Drain water from pasta.

4. Put pasta, tomatoes with oil, garlic, and 1/4 teaspoon salt in a large serving bowl. Lift with tongs or two forks and toss to coat. Add Parmesan cheese and toss again. Scatter ricotta salata slivers over the pasta. Season with pepper and serve immediately.

Oven-Dried Cherry Tomatoes

The concentrated tomato flavor of oven-dried cherry tomatoes tastes so good, you'll want to toss them into salads, pasta, or serve them on crostini. This method is particularly good for preparing cherry tomatoes when tomatoes are plentiful and cheap. After drying and cooling the tomatoes, pack them in olive oil and store in the refrigerator for up to 1 month.

Penne With Spinach, Beans, and Garlic

This simple dish of greens, beans, and pasta is filling and delicious.

1. Bring 4 quarts of water to a boil in a large covered pot. Add 2 teaspoons salt, if you like. Add pasta, stir, and partially cover the pot until water returns to a boil. Immediately remove cover, stir again, and cook pasta just until al dente. Just before draining, ladle out 1/3 cup pasta water and reserve. Drain remaining water from pasta and return to covered pot, off the heat, if sauce is not ready.

2. Heat oil, garlic, and red pepper flakes in a large nonstick skillet set over medium heat. Cook, stirring, until garlic releases its aroma, about 2 minutes. Add spinach and reserved cooking water to skillet. Cover and cook until spinach wilts, 2 to 3 minutes. Reduce heat to low.

3. Add beans and pasta to skillet. Lift with tongs or two forks and toss until heated through, about 2 minutes. Stir in cheese. Season to taste with salt and pepper.

12 OUNCES PENNE

2 TABLESPOONS OLIVE OIL

2 TABLESPOONS MINCED OR PRESSED GARLIC

1/2 TEASPOON CRUSHED RED PEPPER FLAKES

2 LARGE BUNCHES SPINACH, STEMS REMOVED, RINSED WELL, AND DRAINED

1 CAN (15 OUNCES) CANNELLINI (WHITE KIDNEY BEANS), RINSED AND DRAINED

1/3 CUP FRESHLY GRATED PARMESAN CHEESE

SALT AND FRESHLY GROUND BLACK PEPPER, TO TASTE

SERVES 4

Vegetable Primer

Before you cook leafy greens, fill the sink with enough cool water to cover the greens completely. Let the leaves sit for a few minutes, then swish them in the water several times. Lift greens from the water, leaving the grit and uninvited insects behind, and put them in a colander. Shake to remove excess water. Drain water from sink and repeat until water runs clear. Follow recipe directions for cooking.

Orecchiette with Swiss chard and Feta cheese

You can substitute spinach, kale, or any other dark leafy green vegetable for the chard.

12 OUNCES ORECCHIETTE

3 TABLESPOONS OLIVE OIL

4 SHALLOTS, FINELY CHOPPED

1 POUND SWISS CHARD, RINSED, DRAINED, STALKS REMOVED, AND LEAVES COARSELY CHOPPED

1/4 CUP (2 OUNCES) FETA CHEESE, CRUMBLED

SALT AND FRESHLY GROUND BLACK PEPPER, TO TASTE

SERVES 4

1. Bring 4 quarts of water to a boil in a large covered pot. Add 2 teaspoons salt, if you like. Add pasta, stir, and partially cover the pot until water returns to a boil. Immediately remove cover, stir again, and cook pasta just until al dente. Just before draining, ladle out 1/2 cup pasta water and reserve. Drain remaining water from pasta and return to covered pot, off the heat, if sauce is not ready.

2. While pasta cooks, heat oil in a large skillet over medium heat. Add shallots and cook, stirring, for 1 to 2 minutes, until shallots begin to brown. Add Swiss chard and toss to coat with oil. Cover and cook for 2 minutes, until Swiss chard wilts. Add reserved pasta water.

3. Add pasta to skillet. Over low heat, lift with tongs or two forks and toss to coat for 1 minute. Add feta cheese and toss again. Season to taste with salt and pepper. Serve at once.

Penne Rigati with Sautéed Artichoke, Arugula, and Garlic

This fast and flavorful pasta looks pretty too.

1. Bring 4 quarts of water to a boil in a large covered pot. Add 2 teaspoons salt, if you like. Add pasta, stir, and partially cover the pot until water returns to a boil. Immediately remove cover, stir again, and cook pasta just until al dente. Just before draining, ladle out 1/3 cup pasta water and reserve. Drain remaining water from pasta and return to covered pot, off the heat, if sauce is not ready.

2. While pasta cooks, heat oil and garlic in a medium-size non-reactive skillet over medium heat. Cook, stirring, until garlic releases its aroma, about 2 minutes. Add artichokes and cook, stirring occasionally, until artichokes are heated through, about 3 minutes. Add lemon juice, arugula, and reserved pasta water. Stir to mix. Cover skillet and cook just until arugula wilts, about 1 minute.

3. Add pasta to skillet. Season with salt and pepper to taste. Over low heat, toss for 1 minute with tongs or two forks until heated through. Pass a vegetable peeler over the surface of a chunk of room-temperature Parmesan cheese to create 1/4 cup of thin slivers. Sprinkle the slivers over the pasta and serve immediately.

12 OUNCES PENNE RIGATI

3 TABLESPOONS EXTRA-VIRGIN OLIVE OIL

2 TABLESPOONS MINCED OR PRESSED GARLIC

2 PACKAGES (9 OUNCES EACH) FROZEN ARTICHOKE HEARTS, THAWED AND SLICED

2 TABLESPOONS FRESH LEMON JUICE

2 BUNCHES ARUGULA, WASHED, STEMS TRIMMED, LEAVES TORN INTO STRIPS

SALT AND FRESHLY GROUND BLACK PEPPER, TO TASTE

PARMESAN CHEESE

SERVES 4

Saffron-Flavored Orzo With Vegetables

2 1/4 CUPS CHICKEN BROTH, OR WATER

1/8 TEASPOON SAFFRON THREADS,
   OR A PINCH OF POWDERED
   SAFFRON

1 CUP ORZO

1 RED BELL PEPPER, DICED

1 MEDIUM ZUCCHINI, DICED

1 CUP SMALL BROCCOLI FLORETS

3 TABLESPOONS CHOPPED CILANTRO

SERVES 6

Combine broth and saffron in a covered saucepan. Bring mixture to a boil over medium heat. Stir in orzo, bell pepper, zucchini, and broccoli. Reduce heat, cover, and simmer until orzo absorbs liquid, about 10 minutes. Remove pan from heat and let stand 5 minutes. Add cilantro and fluff orzo with a fork. Serve immediately.

Note: *Cook 10 ounces shelled and deveined shrimp until tender in 2 quarts lightly salted boiling water. Add shrimp when you fluff orzo and toss gently.*

About Saffron

Saffron is made up of the stigmas—the flower parts that catch pollen—of the crocus flower. Approximately 13,000 stigmas are needed to make up 1 ounce of saffron, and 1 plant can contribute just 3 stigmas! Saffron costs plenty, but its distinctive flavor is worth every dollar. Also a dye, saffron will turn pasta yellow when added to the cooking water. If adding color, not flavor, is your primary goal, replace saffron with a pinch or two of the less expensive spice turmeric.

Linguine With Creamy Goat Cheese Pesto

The combination of spinach, walnuts, and goat cheese tastes divine.

1. Bring 4 quarts of water to a boil in a large covered pot. Add 2 teaspoons salt, if you like. Add pasta, stir, and partially cover the pot until water returns to a boil. Immediately remove cover, stir again, and cook pasta just until al dente. Just before draining, ladle out 1/3 cup pasta water and reserve. Drain remaining water from pasta and return to covered pot, off the heat, if sauce is not ready.

2. While pasta cooks, purée spinach and walnuts in a food processor until almost smooth. Add oil and broth and purée until creamy. Scrape mixture into a large serving bowl and stir in the garlic. Add the goat cheese and reserved cooking water. Mash and stir pesto mixture until smooth and evenly blended.

3. Add pasta to pesto. Lift with tongs or two forks and toss to coat. Scatter sun-dried tomatoes over top, if you like. Serve immediately.

12 OUNCES LINGUINE

1 CUP PACKED SPINACH, STEMMED, RINSED, AND COARSELY CHOPPED

1 TABLESPOON TOASTED WALNUTS (SEE PAGE 85)

1 TABLESPOON EXTRA-VIRGIN OLIVE OIL

5 TABLESPOONS CHICKEN OR VEGETABLE BROTH

2 GARLIC CLOVES, MINCED OR PRESSED

3 TABLESPOONS SOFT, MILD GOAT CHEESE

2 TABLESPOONS CHOPPED OIL-PACKED SUN-DRIED TOMATOES (OPTIONAL)

SERVES 4

PASTABILITIES

Combine 1 stick softened unsalted butter with grated zest of 2 lemons, 1 minced garlic clove, and 1/4 cup chopped parsley. Scrape butter onto a piece of plastic wrap, form into a log-shaped roll, wrap tightly, and freeze. Serve a few thin slices on top of each portion of steaming hot pasta when you don't have time to fix a sauce. Serve with plenty of Parmesan cheese.

Tortellini With Fresh Herbs and Sun-Dried Tomatoes

This recipe is one of my summertime favorites. Combine herbs or use just one. Any combination is a winner!

1 CUP CHOPPED FRESH HERBS, SUCH AS
    BASIL, OREGANO, OR PARSLEY
1/4 CUP SUN-DRIED TOMATOES,
    COARSELY CHOPPED (SEE NOTE)
2 GARLIC CLOVES, MINCED OR PRESSED
2 TABLESPOONS OLIVE OIL
12 OUNCES CHEESE TORTELLINI
FRESHLY GRATED PARMESAN CHEESE

SERVES 4 TO 6

1. In a large serving bowl, combine herbs, sun-dried tomatoes, garlic, and olive oil. Mix well.

2. Bring 4 quarts of water to a boil in a large covered pot. Add 2 teaspoons salt, if you like. Add pasta, stir, and partially cover the pot until water returns to a boil. Immediately remove cover, stir again, and cook pasta just until al dente. Just before draining, ladle out 1/4 cup pasta water and pour over herb mixture. Drain remaining water from pasta.

3. Add pasta to herb mixture. Lift with tongs or two forks and toss to coat. Sprinkle with Parmesan cheese.

Note: *Sun-dried tomatoes should be soaked for 20 minutes before chopping if dry-packed.*

SUN-DRIED TOMATOES

The tart-sweet flavor of sun-dried tomatoes perks up the taste of many pasta dishes. Sun-dried tomatoes are available two ways, either packed dry or in oil, and are usually shelved with other Italian specialties in the supermarket, or sometimes at the deli counter. Oil-packed tomatoes are convenient to use, but they're more expensive and saltier than the dry-packed variety. If you like, use the oil sparingly to season savory dishes.

Soak dry-packed tomatoes before using. Drop them into a large pot of boiling water for 10 minutes, and cook until soft. Drain the liquid from the tomatoes. Using tongs, spread the tomatoes on a cookie rack or large plate to cool. When cool enough to handle, arrange tomatoes on a double layer of paper towels, blotting excess moisture. Allow to dry thoroughly. If not using right away, layer tomatoes loosely in jars and add olive oil just to cover. Seal tightly and store in the refrigerator.

Spaghetti With Zucchini and Mint

Shred zucchini in a food processor or on the widest side of a hand grater.

1. Bring 4 quarts of water to a boil in a large covered pot. Add 2 teaspoons salt, if you like. Add pasta, stir, and partially cover the pot until water returns to a boil. Immediately remove cover, stir again, and cook pasta just until al dente. Drain water from pasta and return to covered pot, off the heat.

2. While pasta cooks, heat olive oil in a large nonstick skillet over medium-high heat. Add zucchini and garlic and cook until zucchini begins to brown, 4 to 5 minutes. Season to taste with salt and pepper. Add lemon juice and mint, stir, and remove from heat.

3. Add sauce to pasta. Lift with tongs or two forks and toss to coat. Add Parmesan cheese and toss again. Serve at once.

12 OUNCES SPAGHETTI OR LINGUINE

2 TABLESPOONS OLIVE OIL

4 TO 6 SMALL ZUCCHINI, SHREDDED

3 LARGE GARLIC CLOVES, MINCED OR PRESSED

SALT AND FRESHLY GROUND BLACK PEPPER, TO TASTE

3 TABLESPOONS FRESH LEMON JUICE

2 TEASPOONS CHOPPED FRESH MINT LEAVES

2 TABLESPOONS FRESHLY GRATED PARMESAN CHEESE

SERVES 4

Farfalle with Peas, Scallions, and Mint

You can pull this pasta together quickly.

8 OUNCES FARFALLE

2 TABLESPOONS BUTTER

4 OUNCES PANCETTA, CUT INTO
   1/4-INCH DICE

1 CUP CHICKEN OR VEGETABLE BROTH

1 PACKAGE (10 OUNCES) FROZEN TINY
   PEAS, THAWED

2 SCALLIONS, THINLY SLICED, INCLUD-
   ING GREEN AND WHITE PARTS

1/4 CUP MINCED FRESH MINT LEAVES

SALT AND FRESHLY GROUND BLACK
   PEPPER, TO TASTE

SERVES 4

1. Bring 4 quarts of water to a boil in a large covered pot. Add 2 teaspoons salt, if you like. Add pasta, stir, and partially cover the pot until water returns to a boil. Immediately remove cover, stir again, and cook pasta just until al dente. Drain water from pasta and return to pot, off the heat, if sauce is not ready.

2. While pasta cooks, melt butter in a medium skillet over low heat. Add pancetta and stir constantly for 1 minute, until browned. Add broth and heat to boiling over high heat, scraping off any brown bits from bottom of skillet. Boil for 2 minutes. Add thawed peas, scallions, mint, and salt and pepper to taste. Reduce heat, cover, and simmer mixture until peas are tender, about 3 minutes. Remove from heat.

3. Add the pasta to the sauce. Over low heat, lift with tongs or two forks and toss for 1 minute, until heated through. Serve immediately.

Noodles With Peppered Cottage Cheese

My mother made these yummy noodles weekly when I was growing up, and now my family enjoys them just as often. You'll want to make this recipe part of your repertoire too.

1. Remove cottage cheese from refrigerator just before heating water for pasta. Set aside.

2. Bring 4 quarts of water to a boil in a large covered pot. Add 2 teaspoons of salt, if you like. Add noodles, stir, and partially cover the pot until water returns to a boil. Immediately remove cover, stir again, and cook noodles just until al dente. Drain water from noodles and return to pot, off the heat.

3. Add cottage cheese to noodles. Lift with tongs or two forks and toss once or twice. Cover pot and let stand for 1 to 2 minutes, until cheese melts slightly. Season with salt and plenty of pepper and toss again. Serve immediately.

12 OUNCES CURLY WIDE NOODLES
1 CONTAINER (16 OUNCES) LOW-FAT
    COTTAGE CHEESE (ABOUT 1 3/4
    CUPS)
SALT AND FRESHLY GROUND BLACK
    PEPPER, TO TASTE

SERVES 4

Vidalia Onions with Cabbage and Noodles

If you can't find Vidalia onions, use whatever yellow onions you have on hand.

8 OUNCES WIDE NOODLES
2 OUNCES SLICED BACON (ABOUT 2
  SLICES), CUT INTO 1/2-INCH PIECES
1 TABLESPOON OLIVE OIL
1 CUP CHOPPED VIDALIA ONION
1/2 CUP CHICKEN, BEEF, OR
  VEGETABLE BROTH
1 SMALL HEAD GREEN CABBAGE (ABOUT
  1 1/2 POUNDS), FINELY SHREDDED
1 TEASPOON CARAWAY SEEDS
SALT AND FRESHLY GROUND PEPPER,
  TO TASTE

SERVES 4 TO 6

1. Bring 4 quarts of water to a boil in a large covered pot. Add 2 teaspoons of salt, if you like. Add noodles, stir, and partially cover the pot until water returns to a boil. Immediately remove cover, stir again, and cook noodles just until al dente. Drain water from noodles and return to covered pot, off the heat, if sauce is not ready.

2. While the noodles cook, cook the bacon in a large skillet over medium heat until all fat is rendered. Remove bacon to a layer of paper towels and pat well to remove remaining fat. Discard fat from skillet and wipe out the skillet with a paper towel. Add oil and onion. Cover and cook, stirring occasionally, for 10 minutes, or until onion is translucent. Add broth and scrape off any brown bits from bottom of skillet. Add cabbage. Cover and cook until crisp-tender, about 8 minutes.

3. Add drained noodles and caraway seeds to cabbage. Over low heat, lift with tongs or two forks and toss to coat for 1 minute, until heated through. Season to taste with salt and pepper. Serve immediately.

Onions: Nothing to Cry Over

A world without onions? No way! But weep no more when you choose one of the following:

- Freeze onions for about 30 minutes before slicing
- Peel and cut onion from the top, leaving the root end intact
- Wear contact lenses while you peel or cut!

Lemon Poppy Seed Noodles

My family is particularly fond of poppy seeds, and I very often serve this pasta alongside grilled or broiled chicken. Purchase small quantities of the freshest poppy seeds available and use as soon as possible, since they lose their flavor over time.

1. Bring 4 quarts of water to a boil in a large covered pot. Add 2 teaspoons salt, if you like. Add pasta, stir, and partially cover the pot until water returns to a boil. Immediately remove cover, stir again, and cook pasta just until al dente. Drain water from pasta and return to pot, off the heat.

2. While pasta cooks, warm oil, lemon juice, garlic, and salt in a small saucepan over medium heat, stirring, until garlic gives off its aroma, about 1 minute. Stir in poppy seeds and remove from heat.

3. Pour poppy seed mixture over pasta. Lift with tongs or two forks and toss to coat. Serve immediately.

8 OUNCES ROTINI OR BOW TIES
2 TABLESPOONS EXTRA-VIRGIN OLIVE
    OIL
2 TABLESPOONS FRESH LEMON JUICE
2 GARLIC CLOVES, MINCED OR PRESSED
1/4 TEASPOON SALT
1 TABLESPOON POPPY SEEDS

SERVES 4

PASTA
with Seafood

I can't think of more complementary companions than pasta and seafood. Each cooks quickly, provides delicious taste, and lends itself to a variety of flavors and sauces.

Think "3-S" when buying fresh fish and shellfish. Purchase fish that smells *sweet*, looks *shiny*, and feels *springy* when touched. If you're buying frozen fish, purchase only solidly frozen and glossy-looking fish. Any sign of "snow" in the package indicates that the fish thawed and was refrozen.

Sautéed Scallops with Tomato, Lime, and Cilantro

8 OUNCES ANGEL HAIR PASTA

8 OUNCES BAY SCALLOPS

2 TABLESPOONS OLIVE OIL

1 GARLIC CLOVE, MINCED OR PRESSED

1 RIPE MEDIUM TOMATO, DICED

2 TABLESPOONS FRESH LIME JUICE

1/4 CUP MINCED FRESH CILANTRO OR
PARSLEY

SALT AND FRESHLY GROUND BLACK
PEPPER, TO TASTE

SERVES 4

1. Bring 4 quarts of water to a boil in a large covered pot. Add 2 teaspoons salt, if you like. Add pasta, stir, and partially cover the pot until water returns to a boil. Immediately remove cover, stir again, and cook pasta just until al dente. Drain water from pasta and return to covered pot, off the heat, if sauce is not ready.

2. While pasta cooks, rinse scallops under cold water, then drain and pat dry. Heat oil in a medium skillet over medium-high heat until almost smoking. Add scallops and cook for 2 minutes. Turn scallops and sauté 2 minutes longer. Remove from heat and stir in garlic, diced tomato, lime juice, cilantro, and salt and pepper to taste.

3. Add pasta to sauce. Lift with tongs or two forks and toss to combine. Serve immediately.

Spaghetti with Shrimp

If you use medium shrimp in this recipe, add 2 additional shrimp for each portion.

1. Bring 4 quarts of water to a boil in a large covered pot. Add 2 teaspoons salt, if you like. Add pasta, stir, and partially cover the pot until water returns to a boil. Immediately remove cover, stir again, and cook pasta just until al dente. Drain water from pasta and return to covered pot, off the heat, if sauce is not ready.

2. While pasta cooks, heat oil in a large skillet over medium-high heat. Add garlic and cook for 30 seconds. Add white wine. Reduce heat and simmer for 2 minutes. Add tomatoes, thyme, and salt. Heat to boiling, while stirring and breaking up tomatoes with back of spoon. Reduce heat and simmer, uncovered, until most of the liquid has evaporated, 5 minutes. Add shrimp, cover, and simmer for 4 to 5 minutes, until shrimp become pink and opaque. Transfer shrimp to a small bowl and remove skillet from heat.

3. Add pasta to sauce. Over low heat, lift with tongs or two forks and toss to coat for 1 minute. Divide pasta among 4 heated serving bowls. Arrange 3 shrimp on each serving and scatter parsley over top. Serve immediately.

12 OUNCES SPAGHETTI
1 TABLESPOON OLIVE OIL
2 GARLIC CLOVES, MINCED OR PRESSED
1/2 CUP DRY WHITE WINE
2 CANS (28 OUNCES EACH) ITALIAN-STYLE PLUM TOMATOES, DRAINED
1 TEASPOON DRIED THYME
1/8 TEASPOON SALT
12 LARGE SHRIMP, PEELED AND DEVEINED
1 TABLESPOON CHOPPED FRESH PARSLEY

SERVES 4

Horseradish-Crumb-Crusted Salmon with Tagliolini and Tomato Coulis

Serve a sorbet or ice cream for dessert.

2 TEASPOONS OLIVE OIL

2 GARLIC CLOVES, MINCED OR PRESSED

1 CAN (28 OUNCES) ITALIAN-STYLE
    PLUM TOMATOES, DRAINED AND
    PURÉED

1 TEASPOON DRIED OREGANO

SALT AND FRESHLY GROUND BLACK
    PEPPER, TO TASTE

16 OUNCES TAGLIOLINI

2 TABLESPOONS PREPARED HORSE-
    RADISH, DRAINED

2 TABLESPOONS LIGHT MAYONNAISE

3 TABLESPOONS BREAD CRUMBS

3 SALMON STEAKS, ABOUT 1 INCH THICK

WATERCRESS SPRIGS FOR GARNISH

SERVES 4

1. Heat oil and garlic together in a medium skillet over medium heat until garlic just turns golden, about 1 minute. Add tomato purée and simmer, uncovered, stirring occasionally, until reduced slightly, about 5 minutes. Add oregano and salt and pepper to taste. Simmer for 8 to 10 minutes, until sauce reduces to about one half. Cover and remove from heat.

2. Preheat oven to 425°F.

3. Bring 4 quarts of water to a boil in a large covered pot. Add 2 teaspoons salt, if you like. Add pasta, stir, and partially cover the pot until water returns to a boil. Immediately remove cover, stir again, and cook pasta just until al dente. Drain water from pasta and return to covered pot, off the heat.

4. In a small bowl, mix horseradish and mayonnaise until blended. Season bread crumbs with 1/4 teaspoon salt and pepper to taste. Brush one side of each salmon steak with horseradish mixture and sprinkle with 1 tablespoon bread crumbs. Arrange salmon on rack of a shallow pan. Bake until salmon tests almost done, about 15 minutes. It should be somewhat pink inside. Remove pan from oven and heat broiler. Broil salmon until crust is browned, 2 to 3 minutes.

5. Add the sauce to the pasta and toss for about 30 seconds over low heat, until heated through. Transfer pasta to a large shallow serving bowl. Cut salmon into chunks and add to pasta. Garnish with watercress. Serve at once.

Fettuccine With Fresh Tomatoes, Shrimp, and Basil

I never tire of the taste of fresh basil.

1. Bring 4 quarts of water to a boil in a large covered pot. Add 2 teaspoons salt, if you like. Add pasta, stir, and partially cover the pot until water returns to a boil. Immediately remove cover, stir again, and cook pasta just until al dente. Drain water from pasta and return to covered pot, off the heat.

2. Meanwhile heat oil, garlic, and onion in a large nonstick skillet over medium-high heat, about 1 minute. Add tomatoes and chopped basil. Cover and cook for 3 to 4 minutes, until bubbly. Add shrimp and cook uncovered for 2 to 3 minutes, stirring frequently, until shrimp turn pink and opaque. Remove from heat.

3. Add the sauce to the pasta and season to taste with salt and pepper. Garnish each serving with fresh basil leaves and serve at once.

12 OUNCES FETTUCCINE

1 TABLESPOON OLIVE OIL

3 LARGE GARLIC CLOVES, MINCED OR PRESSED

2 TABLESPOONS MINCED ONION

4 LARGE RIPE PLUM TOMATOES, SEEDED AND COARSELY CHOPPED

1/2 CUP CHOPPED FRESH BASIL, PLUS WHOLE LEAVES FOR GARNISH

1 POUND MEDIUM SHRIMP, PEELED AND DEVEINED, TAILS LEFT ON

SALT AND FRESHLY GROUND BLACK PEPPER, TO TASTE

SERVES 4

How to Peel and Seed Tomatoes

Peeling and seeding tomatoes is not always a priority for me, and I often disregard those directions. This is an easy way to peel, if you prefer them skinless.

Cut away the core and slash an X in one end. Plunge the tomato(es) into rapidly boiling water two at a time if you're doing more than one for 15 to 20 seconds, or just until the skin begins to curl away from the X. The riper the tomato, the less time required. Use a slotted spoon to remove the tomatoes from the boiling water and rinse once under cold water. When the tomatoes are cool enough to handle, use your fingers or a sharp knife to strip away the loosened skin. Cut the tomato in half lengthwise and scoop out the seeds with the tip of a small spoon.

Grilled Tuna With Ginger-Flavored Noodles

Although best if made just before serving, the tuna for this flavorful, colorful salad can be made a day in advance with great success.

8 OUNCES BUCKWHEAT NOODLES

1 POUND FRESH TUNA, CUT INTO SLICES APPROXIMATELY 1/2 INCH THICK

OLIVE OIL FOR BRUSHING TUNA SLICES

1 SMALL CUCUMBER, PEELED, SEEDED, AND CUT INTO PAPER-THIN HALF MOONS

2 SCALLIONS, CUT INTO THIN STRIPS, BOTH WHITE AND GREEN PART

2 BELL PEPPERS, RED OR YELLOW, SEEDED AND CUT INTO THIN STRIPS

2/3 CUP RICE WINE VINEGAR

2 TABLESPOONS REDUCED-SALT SOY SAUCE

1 TABLESPOON OLIVE OIL

1 TABLESPOON SESAME OIL

2 TABLESPOONS SHREDDED FRESH GINGER

2 TEASPOONS TOASTED SESAME SEEDS

SERVES 4

1. Bring 4 quarts of water to a boil in a large covered pot. Add noodles, stir, and bring water to a simmer. Cover the pot and simmer until noodles are almost tender, about 5 minutes. Drain water from the noodles. Plunge noodles into cool water to stop the cooking. Drain again. Put noodles in a large serving bowl and set aside.

2. Brush the tuna slices lightly with olive oil. Cook on a hot outdoor grill or in a preheated broiler for about 3 minutes per side. Do not overcook, as the fish will continue to cook for 1 to 2 minutes even after you remove it from the heat. Transfer tuna to a chopping board and cool to room temperature. Cut slices into 1-inch chunks. Add tuna, cucumber, scallions, and peppers to noodles in serving bowl. Lift with tongs or two forks and gently toss to mix.

3. Combine rice wine vinegar, soy sauce, olive oil, sesame oil, ginger, and sesame seeds in a small bowl and whisk together until thoroughly blended. Pour dressing over salad. Lift with tongs or two forks and toss well.

Fettuccine with Smoked Salmon and Asparagus

1. Heat oil in a large skillet over medium heat. Add asparagus and cook for 3 minutes. Add shallots and continue to cook for 3 minutes, stirring occasionally, until shallots soften but do not brown. Add skim milk and half-and-half. Heat mixture and simmer for 5 to 7 minutes, stirring occasionally, until sauce thickens slightly. Remove from heat.

2. Bring 4 quarts of water to a boil in a large covered pot. Add 2 teaspoons salt, if you like. Add pasta, stir, and partially cover the pot until water returns to a boil. Immediately remove cover, stir again, and cook pasta just until al dente. Drain water from pasta and return to covered pot, off the heat.

3. Add the sauce, salmon, and dill to the cooked pasta and toss for 1 to 2 minutes, over low heat, until fettuccine is heated through. Serve immediately.

1 TABLESPOON OLIVE OIL

1/2 POUND FRESH ASPARAGUS, TRIMMED AND CUT INTO 1-INCH PIECES

2 TEASPOONS MINCED SHALLOTS

3/4 CUP SKIM MILK

1/3 CUP HALF-AND-HALF

12 OUNCES FETTUCCINE

4 OUNCES SMOKED SALMON, SLICED 1/4 INCH THICK

2 TABLESPOONS MINCED FRESH DILL

SERVES 4

Shrimp, Sun-Dried Tomatoes, and Creamy Basil Sauce

12 OUNCES FETTUCCINE

2 TEASPOONS OLIVE OIL

3/4 CUP CHOPPED ONION

1/2 CUP COARSELY CHOPPED
SUN-DRIED TOMATOES
(DRY-PACKED; SEE PAGE 94)

2 GARLIC CLOVES, FINELY MINCED OR
PRESSED

1 CUP SKIM MILK

1/3 CUP HALF-AND-HALF

3 TABLESPOONS FRESHLY GRATED
PARMESAN CHEESE

3/4 POUND MEDIUM SHRIMP, SHELLED
AND DEVEINED, TAILS LEFT ON

2 TABLESPOONS CHOPPED FRESH BASIL

SALT AND FRESHLY GROUND BLACK
PEPPER, TO TASTE

SERVES 4

1. Bring 4 quarts of water to a boil in a large covered pot. Add 2 teaspoons salt, if you like. Add pasta, stir, and partially cover the pot until water returns to a boil. Immediately remove cover, stir again, and cook pasta just until al dente. Drain water from pasta and return to covered pot, off the heat, if sauce is not ready.

2. While pasta cooks, heat olive oil, onion, and sun-dried tomatoes in a large skillet over medium heat. Cook, stirring occasionally, for 6 to 8 minutes, until onion softens and turns golden. Add garlic and cook until it releases its aroma. Add skim milk, half-and-half, and Parmesan cheese. Heat to a gentle simmer, then cook for 3 to 4 minutes, until slightly thickened. Add shrimp and basil. Cook and stir, for 2 to 3 minutes, until shrimp turn pink and opaque and are cooked through.

3. Add pasta to sauce. Over low heat, lift with tongs or two forks and toss to coat for 1 minute. Season to taste with salt and pepper. Serve immediately.

Shrimp Shelling Tips

Shell all the shrimp first, before deveining any one of them. Use a small paring knife to split the shells' spine, then remove the shells with your fingers.

Devein shrimp with either a small, beak-shaped paring knife or a shrimp deveiner. This special tool is 4 to 5 inches long, has a curved flat blade, and removes the veins quite easily.

Sautéed Shrimp with Orzo

Serve with a basket of hot crusty bread and a bowl of steamed green beans.

1. Bring 4 quarts of water to a boil in a large covered pot. Add 2 teaspoons salt, if you like. Add orzo, stir, and partially cover the pot until water returns to a boil. Immediately remove cover, stir and cook until al dente. Just before draining, ladle out 1/2 cup pasta water and reserve, if not using broth. Drain remaining water from orzo and return to covered pot.

2. While orzo cooks, heat olive oil and garlic together in a large nonstick skillet over medium-high heat. Stir constantly until garlic releases its aroma, about 1 minute. Add the shrimp, 2 tablespoons parsley, tomatoes, broth, oregano, and salt and pepper to taste. Cook for 5 to 6 minutes longer, stirring constantly, until shrimp turn pink and opaque. Remove skillet from heat. Stir in feta cheese, capers, and remaining parsley.

3. Add shrimp mixture to orzo and toss well. Serve immediately.

1 CUP ORZO
1 TABLESPOON OLIVE OIL
2 GARLIC CLOVES, MINCED OR PRESSED
16 MEDIUM SHRIMP, PEELED AND
    DEVEINED, TAILS LEFT ON
1/4 CUP FINELY CHOPPED PARSLEY
1 1/2 CUPS CHOPPED RIPE PLUM
    TOMATOES
1/2 CUP CHICKEN BROTH OR
    RESERVED COOKING LIQUID
1 TEASPOON DRIED OREGANO
SALT AND FRESHLY GROUND BLACK
    PEPPER, TO TASTE
1/4 CUP CRUMBLED FETA CHEESE
1 TABLESPOON CAPERS, RINSED

SERVES 4

CAPERS

Capers are the flower buds of the *Capparis spinosa* bush, which grows in the Mediterranean. Capers are typically cured in either salt or vinegar, so rinse them under cold running water before using.

Mussels with Linguine and Spicy Tomatoes

While cleaning mussels takes time, this sauce is too good not to try.

12 OUNCES LINGUINE

1 TABLESPOON OLIVE OIL

1 SMALL ONION, CHOPPED

3 LARGE GARLIC CLOVES, MINCED OR
PRESSED

1/4 TEASPOON CRUSHED RED PEPPER
FLAKES, OR TO TASTE

1 CAN (28 OUNCES) ITALIAN-STYLE
PLUM TOMATOES, DRAINED AND
CHOPPED

1 1/2 TEASPOONS DRIED MARJORAM

1/4 CUP MINCED FRESH PARSLEY

2 POUNDS MUSSELS, RINSED,
SCRUBBED, AND DEBEARDED

SERVES 4

1. Bring 4 quarts of water to a boil in a large covered pot. Add 2 teaspoons salt, if you like. Add pasta, stir, and partially cover the pot until water returns to a boil. Immediately remove cover, stir again, and cook pasta just until al dente. Drain water from pasta and return to pot, off the heat.

2. While pasta cooks, heat together oil, onion, and garlic in a Dutch oven over medium heat. Cook, stirring occasionally, until onion is limp and translucent, 8 minutes. Add red pepper flakes. Cook for 20 seconds, stirring constantly. Add tomatoes and simmer for 5 minutes, stirring frequently, until sauce thickens. Stir in marjoram and half the parsley. Add mussels. Cover and cook until mussels open, 6 to 8 minutes. Transfer opened mussels to pasta, discarding any mussels that remain closed. Slowly pour the sauce over the pasta, leave the sandy sediment at the bottom of the pot. Sprinkle with remaining chopped parsley. Serve immediately.

Buying and Storing Mussels

Buy only fresh, tightly closed mussels or, if opened, only those that snap shut when lightly tapped. Cook them immediately, or pack them in ice in a large stainless steel bowl. Store mussels in the coldest part of the refrigerator for up to 12 hours, adding more ice cubes if necessary to keep them completely covered with ice. Clean mussels just before cooking to remove grit or barnacles. Scrub the shells with a wire brush under cold running water and to debeard, pull the coarse, tangled fibers out of the shell with your fingertips. Rinse several times under cold running water, then cook immediately.

PASTA

with Poultry or Meat

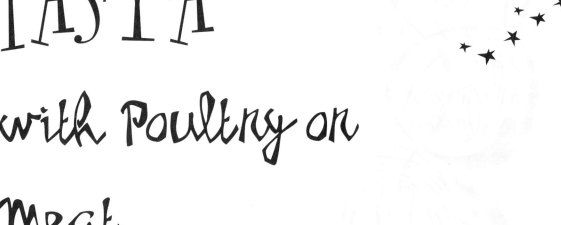

Poultry and pasta blend with a wide variety of spices and sauces. If you use quick-cooking cuts, such as boneless, skinless poultry breasts, ground poultry, and poultry sausages, dinner is done in no more time than it takes to boil the pasta.

The same holds true for meat and pasta. What's more, you cut costs as well as fat when you combine a mere 2 or 3 ounces of meat with pasta. Lean cuts that cook the fastest include ground beef, pork, and veal. You can also cook a few strips of bacon until very crisp, pat on paper towels to absorb excess fat, dice, and stir into the sauce. When cooked until the fat is rendered, small amounts of bacon or pancetta contribute lots of flavor without adding too many calories.

Smoky Tomatoes and Chili over Pasta

A shallot is a type of mild onion that looks similar to garlic. If necessary, substitute an equal amount of onion. Broiling the tomatoes until charred gives this chili its rich, smoky taste.

2 POUNDS (ABOUT 8) LARGE RIPE PLUM
    TOMATOES
1 TABLESPOON CANOLA OIL
1/2 CUP CHOPPED SHALLOTS
1 POUND GROUND TURKEY
SALT AND FRESHLY GROUND BLACK
    PEPPER, TO TASTE
2 TABLESPOONS CHILI POWDER
1/2 TEASPOON EACH PAPRIKA,
    OREGANO, AND CUMIN
2 TABLESPOONS TOMATO PASTE
1 CAN (16 OUNCES) RED KIDNEY BEANS,
    RINSED AND DRAINED
16 OUNCES SPAGHETTI
1/4 CUP GRATED WHITE CHEDDAR
    CHEESE

SERVES 6

1. Preheat broiler. Core and cut tomatoes in half lengthwise. Place tomatoes cut side down on an aluminum-lined broiler pan and broil until skins completely char, 12 to 15 minutes. Remove the pan from the broiler and pull off the skins with a fork. Discard the skins.

2. Meanwhile, heat the oil for 30 seconds in a large nonstick skillet over medium-high heat. Add the shallots and cook, stirring until soft and translucent, about 3 minutes. Crumble the ground turkey into the skillet, season to taste with salt and pepper, and cook, stirring, until turkey and shallots are lightly browned, about 5 minutes. Add the chili powder and cook, stirring to coat the meat, about 1 minute. Add the tomatoes, paprika, oregano, cumin, tomato paste, kidney beans, plus 1/2 to 1 cup water. Bring the mixture to a boil, stirring to break up the tomatoes with the back of a wooden spoon. Reduce heat to medium-low and simmer, covered, for 20 minutes, stirring occasionally. Taste and adjust seasonings if necessary.

3. While the chili cooks, bring 4 quarts of water to a boil in a large covered pot. Add 2 teaspoons salt if you like. Add pasta, stir, and partially cover the pot until water returns to a boil. Immediately remove cover, stir again, and cook spaghetti just until al dente. Drain and pile pasta into 6 bowls. Spoon chili on top. Sprinkle with Cheddar cheese. Serve immediately.

Pasta With Turkey Sausage and Mushrooms

1. Bring 4 quarts of water to a boil in a large covered pot. Add 2 teaspoons salt, if you like. Add pasta, stir, and partially cover the pot until water returns to a boil. Immediately remove cover, stir again, and cook pasta just until al dente. Drain water from pasta and return to covered pot, off the heat.

2. While pasta cooks, crumble sausage into a large nonstick skillet, and cook, stirring often, over medium-high heat, until well browned, 10 minutes. Use a slotted spoon to remove sausage and set aside. Pour off fat from skillet.

3. Return skillet to medium-high heat and add mushrooms. Cook, stirring often, for 4 to 5 minutes, until mushrooms release their liquid. Add garlic and cook, stirring, for 1 to 2 minutes, until mushrooms are browned. Add Madeira all at once. Stir quickly with a wooden spoon, scraping off browned bits from skillet. Add half-and-half, broth, nutmeg, Parmesan cheese, and cooked sausage and bring to a boil. Boil sauce for 2 to 3 minutes, until slightly thickened. Cover skillet and remove from heat.

4. Add pasta to sauce. Over low heat, lift with tongs or two forks and toss to coat for 1 minute. Sprinkle with parsley and toss again. Serve at once.

12 OUNCES PENNE OR RIGATONI

8 OUNCES MILD ITALIAN TURKEY SAUSAGE, CASINGS REMOVED

1/2 POUND BUTTON MUSHROOMS, SLICED

2 LARGE GARLIC CLOVES, MINCED OR PRESSED

1/4 CUP MADEIRA OR DRY SHERRY

1/4 CUP HALF-AND-HALF

1/2 CUP CHICKEN BROTH

1/4 TEASPOON GROUND NUTMEG

1/4 CUP FRESHLY GRATED PARMESAN CHEESE

2 TABLESPOONS CHOPPED FRESH PARSLEY

SERVES 4

Basil Chicken over Noodles

16 OUNCES RIGATONI OR PENNE

12 OUNCES SKINLESS, BONELESS
   CHICKEN BREASTS

SALT AND FRESHLY GROUND BLACK
   PEPPER, TO TASTE

1 TABLESPOON OLIVE OIL

1 ONION, CHOPPED

2 GARLIC CLOVES, MINCED OR PRESSED

1/4 CUP WHITE WINE

2 CUPS CHICKEN BROTH

1 CAN (28 OUNCES) ITALIAN-STYLE
   PLUM TOMATOES

1/2 CUP CHOPPED FRESH BASIL

FRESHLY GRATED PARMESAN CHEESE

FRESH BASIL LEAVES, FOR GARNISH

SERVES 4

1. Bring 4 quarts of water to a boil in a large covered pot. Add 2 teaspoons salt, if you like. Add pasta, stir, and partially cover the pot until water returns to a boil. Immediately remove cover, stir again, and cook pasta just until al dente. Drain water from pasta and return to covered pot.

2. While pasta cooks, season the chicken with salt and pepper to taste. Heat the olive oil in a large skillet over medium-high heat. Add the chicken and cook until meat is no longer pink inside, 2 to 3 minutes per side. Remove chicken, cut into thin strips, and set aside.

3. Add onions and garlic to skillet. Cook, stirring, over low heat, until onion turns translucent, about 5 minutes. Add white wine and bring to a boil, scraping up any brown bits with a wooden spoon. Add the broth, tomatoes and basil and cook, stirring, until mixture returns to a boil. Reduce heat and simmer, uncovered, stirring occasionally, until sauce thickens, about 20 minutes. Remove from heat.

4. Add chicken and sauce to pasta. Over low heat, lift with tongs or two forks and toss for 1 minute, until heated through. Transfer pasta to a large serving bowl. Sprinkle Parmesan cheese over top and garnish with basil leaves. Serve immediately.

Pulling Pasta From the Pot

In Italy, the practice of draining pasta is virtually unheard of. Instead, cooks "pull out" the pasta from the cooking water, preserving its light starchy coating. This little bit of starch tastes good and helps the sauce "sit" on the pasta. A toothed pasta server or tongs safely removes long pasta strands, and a large, almost flat, Chinese-style perforated spoon works best for short pasta shapes.

Lasagne noodles, large shells, and pasta destined for salads are the only exceptions to this rule. These pastas *should* be drained, dunked into a bowl of cold water, and then drained again before using. The plunge prevents the noodles and shells from sticking together. It also stops the cooking process for pasta intended for salads.

Pasta With Turkey Sausage and Broccoli Rabe

1 POUND LINGUINE OR SPAGHETTI

*12 OUNCES SWEET ITALIAN TURKEY
SAUSAGE, CASING REMOVED*

1 TABLESPOON OLIVE OIL

3 GARLIC CLOVES, MINCED OR PRESSED

1 CUP CHICKEN BROTH

*1 BUNCH FRESH BROCCOLI RABE (ABOUT
1 1/2 POUNDS), WASHED, TRIMMED,
AND CUT INTO 2-INCH PIECES*

*1/4 TEASPOON CRUSHED RED PEPPER
FLAKES*

FRESHLY GRATED PARMESAN CHEESE

SERVES 6

1. Bring 4 quarts of water to a boil in a large covered pot. Add 2 teaspoons salt, if you like. Add pasta, stir, and partially cover the pot until water returns to a boil. Immediately remove cover, stir again, and cook pasta just until al dente. Drain water from pasta and return to covered pot, off the heat.

2. While pasta cooks, heat a large nonstick skillet over medium heat. Crumble sausage into skillet and cook, stirring, for 5 to 6 minutes, until lightly browned. Push sausage to side of skillet and add oil and garlic. Cook over medium-high heat, stirring, for about 1 minute, until garlic is golden. Add broth, broccoli rabe, and red pepper flakes. Bring mixture to a boil, then reduce heat, cover, and gently simmer until broccoli rabe is tender, 6 to 7 minutes. Remove from heat.

3. Add pasta to sauce. Over low heat, lift with tongs or two forks and toss to coat for 1 minute. Scatter Parmesan cheese over top and toss again. Serve immediately.

About Broccoli Rabe

Broccoli rabe (also called broccoli rape) is not broccoli at all, but rather a member of the turnip family. Its buds resemble those found on the common broccoli plant, but rabe has many more leaves than buds, and tastes slightly bitter. Rabe is delicious with pasta, as a side dish vegetable, and in soups. Like other leafy greens, it's a terrific source of vitamin C.

To prepare rabe, first remove the stems and separate the leaves and florets. Cut the stems into 2-inch pieces, using tender stems only and discarding the thick, tough ones. Place stems, leaves, and florets in a bowl of cold water and wash carefully, then lift out and place in a colander. Shake out excess water, but do not dry completely.

Spaghetti and Small Meatballs in Tomato Sauce

Seltzer makes these meatballs special.

1. Purée tomatoes with juices in a food processor or blender. Set aside. Heat oil in a 4-quart saucepan over medium-high heat. Add the onion and cook, stirring, until onion turns golden, about 5 minutes. Add garlic and cook, stirring constantly, until garlic releases its aroma. Add puréed tomatoes, tomato paste, oregano, sugar, 1/4 teaspoon salt, and pepper to taste. Heat sauce to a simmer, stirring. Reduce heat to low, cover and simmer.

2. While sauce simmers, whisk together the egg and seltzer in a large bowl. Add bread crumbs, stir to coat, and let stand 5 minutes. Stir in Parmesan cheese, parsley, 1/4 teaspoon salt, and pepper to taste. Crumble beef into mixture. Stir with a large spoon until blended. Shape meat into 30 1 1/4-inch meatballs.

3. Heat oil in a large skillet over medium-high heat until very hot. Add meatballs a few at a time and cook for 4 to 5 minutes, turning occasionally, until browned. Remove with a slotted spoon and place on paper towels to remove excess oil. Immediately transfer to simmering tomato sauce and cook, uncovered, for about 1 hour, until sauce thickens. Taste for seasoning.

4. To serve, bring 4 quarts of water to a boil in a large covered pot. Add 2 teaspoons salt, if you like. Add pasta, stir, and partially cover the pot until water returns to a boil. Immediately remove cover, stir again, and cook pasta just until al dente. Drain the water from the pasta.

5. Put a portion of pasta into each bowl and spoon some meatballs and sauce in the center. Serve immediately, and pass freshly grated Parmesan cheese, if you like.

TOMATO SAUCE

1 CAN (28 OUNCES) ITALIAN-STYLE PEELED PLUM TOMATOES WITH JUICE
1 TABLESPOON OLIVE OIL
1/2 CUP FINELY CHOPPED ONION
1 GARLIC CLOVE, MINCED OR PRESSED
1 TABLESPOON TOMATO PASTE
1/2 TEASPOON DRIED OREGANO
1/2 TEASPOON SUGAR
SALT AND FRESHLY GROUND BLACK PEPPER, TO TASTE

MEATBALLS

1 EGG
1/4 CUP SELTZER
3/4 CUP FINE BREAD CRUMBS
2 TABLESPOONS FRESHLY GRATED PARMESAN CHEESE
2 TABLESPOONS CHOPPED FRESH PARSLEY
SALT AND FRESHLY GROUND BLACK PEPPER, TO TASTE
1 POUND LEAN GROUND BEEF
1 TABLESPOON OLIVE OIL
16 OUNCES SPAGHETTI
FRESHLY GRATED PARMESAN CHEESE

SERVES 4 TO 6

Mexican-Style Pasta

Olé!

1 CUP COMMERCIALLY PREPARED MILD
   CHUNKY SALSA
1 TABLESPOON FRESH LIME JUICE
12 OUNCES LEAN GROUND BEEF
2 TEASPOONS CHILI POWDER
2 TEASPOONS TACO SEASONING MIX
8 OUNCES ELBOW MACARONI
1 CAN (19 OUNCES) PINTO BEANS,
   DRAINED AND RINSED
1 LARGE RIPE TOMATO, CHOPPED
1 MEDIUM GREEN BELL PEPPER, FINELY
   CHOPPED
1/2 CUP (2 OUNCES) SHREDDED
   MONTEREY JACK CHEESE

SERVES 6

1. In a small bowl, stir together salsa and lime juice. Set aside.

2. Crumble ground beef into a large nonstick skillet over medium-high heat. Cook for 9 to 11 minutes, stirring occasionally, until meat is well browned. Add chili powder, taco seasoning mix, and 3/4 cup water. Cook, stirring with a wooden spoon, until mixture comes to a boil. Reduce heat to low and cook, uncovered, for 5 minutes, stirring occasionally.

3. Bring 4 quarts of water to a boil in a large covered pot. Add 2 teaspoons salt, if you like. Add pasta, stir, and partially cover the pot until water returns to a boil. Immediately remove cover, stir again, and cook pasta just until al dente. Drain water from pasta and return to covered pot. Add the pinto beans, chopped tomato, and beef mixture. Stir to mix. Cook over low heat for about 1 minute. Stir in chopped pepper.

4. Transfer macaroni mixture to a large, warm serving platter. Scatter shredded cheese over top. Pass salsa mixture to spoon over servings.

Kitchen Cleanup

Time spent at the sink cleaning up is downright silly, especially when soaking dirty utensils and pans does the job. Fill the sink with soapy water and drop in dirty utensils or saucepans as you go along. You don't have to scrub the starch that forms inside the pasta pot either—instead, while you dine, soak the pot in *cold* water for easy removal later.

Ants on a Tree Trunk

This spicy Sichuan classic gets its funny name from the tiny bits of ground meat scattered throughout the noodles.

1. In a small bowl, stir together soy sauce, sherry, and chicken broth. Set aside.

2. Place noodles in a large bowl and add boiling water to cover. Let stand until noodles are pliable but not soft, about 15 minutes. Drain very well. Cut noodles into 2-inch lengths.

3. Heat oil over high heat in a wok or heavy large skillet. When oil is very hot but not smoking, add scallions, chili paste, and ginger, stirring constantly, for 10 seconds. Crumble ground pork into wok and stir quickly for 3 to 4 minutes, until meat is no longer pink. Quickly stir soy mixture and add to the wok. Heat to a simmer, stirring occasionally, and then add noodles and water chestnuts. Stir to mix. Reduce heat to maintain a gentle simmer and cook, covered, for 3 to 4 minutes, until liquid is almost absorbed. Taste and adjust seasonings with chili paste. Serve at once.

2 TABLESPOONS SOY SAUCE

2 TABLESPOONS DRY SHERRY

2/3 CUP CHICKEN BROTH

4 OUNCES CELLOPHANE NOODLES

1 TABLESPOON PEANUT OIL

1/3 CUP THINLY SLICED SCALLIONS, WHITE AND GREEN PARTS

2 TEASPOONS CHILI PASTE WITH GARLIC

2 TEASPOONS PEELED, MINCED FRESH GINGER

1/2 POUND LEAN GROUND PORK OR OTHER MEAT

1/2 CUP CANNED WATER CHESTNUTS, RINSED, DRAINED, AND SLICED

SERVES 4

Easy Stuffed Shells

1 CAN (32 OUNCES) ITALIAN-STYLE
    PEELED PLUM TOMATOES, WITH
    JUICE
1 TEASPOON SUGAR
SALT AND FRESHLY GROUND BLACK
    PEPPER, TO TASTE
24 JUMBO SHELLS
1/2 POUND GROUND TURKEY
1 CONTAINER (15 OUNCES) PART-SKIM
    RICOTTA CHEESE
1 PACKAGE (10 OUNCES) FROZEN
    CHOPPED SPINACH, THAWED AND
    SQUEEZED DRY
1/8 TEASPOON FRESHLY GROUND
    NUTMEG

SERVES 4 TO 6

1. Purée tomatoes with juices in a food processor or blender. Transfer to a 3-quart saucepan and bring to a boil over medium-high heat. Add sugar and salt and freshly ground pepper to taste. Reduce heat to low, cover, and simmer sauce for 20 minutes. Remove from heat.

2. While sauce simmers, bring 4 quarts of water to a boil in a large covered pot. Add 2 teaspoons salt, if you like. Add pasta, stir, and partially cover the pot until water returns to a boil. Immediately remove cover, stir again, and cook pasta just until al dente. Drain the water from the pasta. Plunge pasta into cool water to stop cooking. Drain again.

3. While pasta cooks, heat a large skillet over medium heat until very hot, but not smoking. Crumble ground turkey into skillet and cook, stirring frequently, for 5 minutes, until juices evaporate and turkey browns. Remove skillet from heat. Add ricotta cheese, spinach, and grated nutmeg and stir to blend.

4. Preheat oven to 375°F. Using a spoon, stuff shells with turkey mixture. Ladle half the sauce into a 13-by-9-inch baking dish. Arrange filled shells in dish. Ladle remaining sauce over shells. Cover baking dish with foil. Bake 40 minutes, or until shells are heated through and sauce is hot and bubbly.

Using Your Noodle

Freeze individual portions of stuffed shells. Remove as you need them and serve on days when you're eating alone, or when everyone needs to eat on his or her own schedule. Don't worry about defrosting the shells—just cover and cook them in a microwave or conventional oven at 375°F until hot and bubbly.

Penne With Spinach, Prosciutto, and Sun-Dried Tomatoes

1. Bring 4 quarts of water to a boil in a large covered pot. Add 2 teaspoons salt, if you like. Add pasta, stir, and partially cover the pot until water returns to a boil. Immediately remove cover, stir again, and cook pasta just until al dente. Drain water from pasta and return to covered pot if sauce is not ready.

2. While pasta cooks, cook prosciutto in a large nonstick skillet over low heat until lightly browned. Drain off fat and wipe skillet dry. Add olive oil and shallots and cook over low heat until shallots soften, about 6 minutes. Stir in garlic and cook for 1 minute. Add sun-dried tomatoes and olives. Stir over medium heat for 3 minutes. Add chopped spinach. Stir until wilted, about 2 minutes. Remove from heat.

3. Add pasta to sauce. Lift with tongs or two forks and toss. Add pepper to taste. Serve with Parmesan cheese.

12 OUNCES PENNE

6 SLICES PROSCIUTTO (ABOUT 2 OUNCES), CUT INTO 1/4-INCH PIECES

2 TABLESPOONS OLIVE OIL

2 TABLESPOONS MINCED SHALLOTS

1 GARLIC CLOVE, MINCED OR PRESSED

1/4 CUP SLIVERED SUN-DRIED TOMATOES (OIL-PACKED), DRAINED AND BLOTTED DRY

2 TABLESPOONS PITTED AND COARSELY CHOPPED IMPORTED BLACK OLIVES

1 LARGE BUNCH FRESH SPINACH, TRIMMED, WASHED, AND COARSELY CHOPPED

FRESHLY GROUND BLACK PEPPER, TO TASTE

FRESHLY GRATED PARMESAN CHEESE

SERVES 4

Pasta With Pancetta, Arugula, and Plum Tomatoes

The combination of pancetta and arugula is one of my favorites.

12 OUNCES BUCATINI OR SPAGHETTI

2 OUNCES PANCETTA OR BACON, FINELY CHOPPED

2 TABLESPOONS OLIVE OIL

4 TO 5 GARLIC CLOVES, MINCED OR PRESSED

2 BUNCHES ARUGULA, RINSED AND TRIMMED, ABOUT 2 CUPS PACKED LEAVES

3 RIPE PLUM TOMATOES, CHOPPED

SALT AND FRESHLY GROUND BLACK PEPPER, TO TASTE

FRESHLY GRATED PARMESAN CHEESE

SERVES 4

1. Bring 4 quarts of water to a boil in a large covered pot. Add 2 teaspoons salt, if you like. Add pasta, stir, and partially cover the pot until water returns to a boil. Immediately remove cover, stir again, and cook pasta just until al dente. Just before draining, ladle out 1/2 cup pasta water. Drain remaining water from pasta and return to covered pot, off the heat, if sauce is not ready.

2. While pasta cooks, cook pancetta in a large nonstick skillet over medium heat until browned and crisp. Add olive oil and garlic. Cook for 1 minute, stirring constantly, until garlic turns golden. Add arugula and continue to cook, stirring, for about 2 minutes. Add chopped tomatoes, 1/4 teaspoon salt, and pepper to taste. Quickly stir in reserved pasta water, then cover and simmer for 3 minutes. Add the pasta. Over low heat, lift with tongs or two forks and toss gently for 1 minute. Serve with Parmesan cheese.

Using Your Noodle

Cured in salt and spices but not smoked, Italian pancetta is a cut of pork like bacon. In a pinch, substitute smoked slab bacon. To remove the smoky flavor, blanch the bacon slices in enough simmering water to cover for 10 minutes. Drain the slices and pat dry before using.

Parsley Perks

Keep plenty of fresh parsley available in the refrigerator to nibble on after or between meals. Parsley is not only a good source of calcium, but also contains a very high level of chlorophyll, which acts as a natural breath freshener.

PASTA
for the kids

Whether it's simple strands of spaghetti or long, squiggly shapes, what kid doesn't like pasta? Not any I know. The problem kids have with pasta has to do with what is served with pasta or even with pasta colors (green is definitely out). We've heard "I'll have mine with butter," all too often, but take heart: The following recipes have been kid-tested and approved. There's still hope.

Red Sauce for Kids

A good mild-tasting sauce for kids with sensitive taste buds.

1/2 CUP FINELY CHOPPED ONION
1 TABLESPOON OLIVE OIL
1 TEASPOON MINCED OR PRESSED
    GARLIC
1 CAN (28 OUNCES) CRUSHED
    TOMATOES
2 TABLESPOONS TOMATO PASTE
2 TEASPOONS DRIED BASIL
3/4 TEASPOON DRIED OREGANO
1 TABLESPOON SUGAR
SALT AND FRESHLY GROUND BLACK
    PEPPER, TO TASTE
16 OUNCES FARTALLE, ROTELLE, OR
    OTHER "FUN" PASTA SHAPE

SERVES 4

1. Heat onion, oil, and garlic in a medium saucepan over medium-high heat. Cook for 4 to 5 minutes, stirring occasionally, until soft. Add crushed tomatoes with their liquid, tomato paste, basil, oregano, and sugar. Stir frequently and heat to boiling. Reduce heat, cover, and simmer for 15 minutes, stirring occasionally. Season to taste with salt and pepper.

2. While sauce cooks, bring 4 quarts of water to a boil in a large covered pot. Add 2 teaspoon salt, if you like. Add pasta, stir, and partially cover the pot until water returns to a boil. Immediately remove cover, stir again, and cook pasta just until al dente. Drain water from pasta and return to covered pot, off the heat.

3. Mound pasta into individual serving bowls and ladle some sauce on top. Serve with cheese, if you like.

Kids Veggie Spring Sauce

If your children (like mine) complain about eating vegetables, serve them this colorful pasta dish. You may be pleasantly surprised to see what they select from their plate.

1. Bring 4 quarts of water to a boil in a large covered pot. Add 2 teaspoons salt, if you like. Add pasta, stir, and partially cover the pot until water returns to a boil. Immediately remove cover, stir again, and cook pasta just until al dente. Just before draining, ladle out 1/2 cup pasta water and reserve. Drain remaining water from pasta and return to covered pot, off the heat.

2. Meanwhile, heat olive oil in a medium skillet over medium-high heat. Add onion and cook until soft, about 5 minutes. Add asparagus and carrots, cover, and cook for 3 minutes. Add red pepper and squash and cook, stirring, until vegetables are tender, 4 to 5 minutes longer. Add half-and-half and reserved pasta water. Simmer, uncovered, for 2 to 3 minutes, until sauce thickens slightly. Remove from heat and stir in cheese.

3. Add sauce to the pasta. Lift with tongs or two forks and toss for about 30 seconds, until heated through. Serve immediately.

12 OUNCES FETTUCCINE OR
  LINGUINE
1 TABLESPOON OLIVE OIL
1 SMALL ONION, FINELY CHOPPED
1 POUND ASPARAGUS, TRIMMED AND
  CUT CROSSWISE INTO 1/2-INCH
  PIECES (ABOUT 2 CUPS)
2 CARROTS, PEELED AND THINLY SLICED
1 SMALL RED BELL PEPPER, DICED
1 SMALL YELLOW SQUASH, HALVED
  LENGTHWISE AND THINLY SLICED
1/2 CUP HALF-AND-HALF
1/4 CUP FRESHLY GRATED PARMESAN
  OR ROMANO CHEESE

SERVES 4 TO 6

Planning Ahead

Frequently stuck for time? Plan ahead. Except for Kids Veggie Spring Sauce, you can prepare the sauces in this chapter in advance and refrigerate or freeze them. To serve, reheat the sauce in a large covered skillet over medium heat and add cooked pasta. Lift with tongs or two forks and toss. Freeze single servings of sauce (about 3/4 cup) for the nights you or the kids have to eat separately.

Fresh Vegetable Noodle Pizza

Selma Kaleck, my husband's aunt, contributed this delicious recipe. Cut the veggies into 1/4-to-1/2-inch dice.

6 OUNCES BROAD NOODLES OR
  RIBBON NOODLES

1/3 CUP CHICKEN BROTH

1 SMALL ZUCCHINI (ABOUT 6 OUNCES),
  DICED

1 SMALL YELLOW SUMMER SQUASH
  (ABOUT 6 OUNCES), DICED

1 LARGE RIPE TOMATO, SEEDED AND
  DICED

1 PACKAGE (10 OUNCES) FROZEN
  CHOPPED SPINACH, THAWED AND
  SQUEEZED DRY

1/2 TEASPOON DRIED OREGANO

SALT AND FRESHLY GROUND BLACK
  PEPPER, TO TASTE

1 TABLESPOON FRESHLY GRATED
  PARMESAN CHEESE

1/2 CUP SHREDDED PART-SKIM
  MOZZARELLA CHEESE

SERVES 4 TO 6

1. Preheat oven to 350°F. Spray 10-inch pie plate with nonstick cooking spray or grease lightly with oil.

2. Bring 4 quarts of water to a boil in a large covered pot. Add 2 teaspoons salt, if you like. Add pasta, stir, and partially cover the pot until water returns to a boil. Immediately remove cover, stir again, and cook pasta just until al dente. Drain water from pasta, shaking the pasta dry. Arrange noodles in oiled plate to form crust.

3. Bring chicken broth to a boil in a large skillet over medium-high heat. Add zucchini and yellow squash, cover, lower heat, and simmer until vegetables are tender, about 8 minutes. Stir in tomato, spinach, oregano, and salt and pepper to taste.

4. Spoon vegetable mixture over noodle "crust." Sprinkle Parmesan and mozzarella cheese evenly over top. Bake on bottom rack of oven for 20 to 25 minutes, or until cheese has melted and pizza is hot. Remove and cut into wedges.

Saucy One-Skillet Pasta and Vegetables

All these good things cooked in one pot, and you won't believe how easy this dish is to make!

1. Heat a large pot over medium-high heat until hot, but not smoking. Crumble ground turkey into pot and stir often for 2 minutes, until browned. Add red pepper and paprika and cook for 2 minutes; stirring constantly. Add tomatoes, broth, and pasta. Stir, cover, and heat to boiling. Reduce heat and simmer for 15 minutes.

2. Add broccoli and cauliflower, but do not stir into sauce. Cover and continue cooking for 10 minutes, until vegetables are crisp-tender. Remove from heat.

3. Meanwhile, toss together parsley, bread crumbs, and Parmesan cheese in a small bowl. Sprinkle parsley mixture over cooked vegetables in the skillet and let sit for 3 minutes before serving.

1/2 POUND LEAN GROUND TURKEY

1 RED BELL PEPPER, SEEDED AND CUT INTO THIN STRIPS

1 TABLESPOON SWEET PAPRIKA

1 CAN (14 1/2 OUNCES) CRUSHED TOMATOES

2 CUPS CHICKEN BROTH

2 CUPS FARFALLE

2 CUPS BROCCOLI FLORETS

1 CUP CAULIFLOWER FLORETS

1/3 CUP CHOPPED FRESH PARSLEY

1/4 CUP SEASONED BREAD CRUMBS

1/4 CUP FRESHLY GRATED PARMESAN CHEESE

SERVES 6

Corkscrews with Soupy Cheese Sauce

When kids prefer their pasta plain with butter, serve them this delicious alternative. This will feed four to six children—fewer if adults are eating too.

8 OUNCES CORKSCREWS OR SPAGHETTI

1 TABLESPOON BUTTER OR
    MARGARINE

1 SMALL CARROT, SHREDDED

1 CUP CHICKEN BROTH

1/4 CUP FRESHLY GRATED PARMESAN
    OR ROMANO CHEESE

SERVES 4

1. Bring 4 quarts of water to a boil in a large covered pot. Add 2 teaspoons salt, if you like. Add pasta, stir, and partially cover the pot until water returns to a boil. Immediately remove cover, stir again, and cook pasta just until al dente. Drain water from pasta and return to covered pot, off the heat.

2. While pasta cooks, melt butter in a medium saucepan over low heat. Add carrot and cook, stirring, for 2 minutes. Add broth and heat to boiling. Remove saucepan from heat. Stir in cheese.

3. Pour sauce over pasta and heat, for 1 minute, stirring constantly. Serve immediately.

PASTA

for Breakfast and Dessert

Who says you can't eat pasta three times a day? Instead of instant oatmeal, start your day with Raisin-Bran Couscous (or Frittata when you have more time). Mom's Noodle Pudding and Creamy Lemon Orzo Pudding are sweet endings to almost any meal, but trust me, they taste yummy for breakfast too.

Raisin-Bran Couscous

Goodbye cereal, hello pasta!

1 CUP SKIM MILK
1/2 CUP COUSCOUS
2 TABLESPOONS OAT BRAN
1 TABLESPOON RAISINS
GROUND CINNAMON (OPTIONAL)

SERVES 2

Heat milk in a small saucepan until tiny bubbles appear around edges. Add couscous, oat bran, and raisins and stir for 30 seconds. Remove from heat. Cover and let stand for 5 minutes. Sprinkle with cinnamon, if you like.

Frittata

1. Bring 3 cups of water to a boil in a medium-sized covered pot. Add 2 teaspoons salt, if you like. Add pasta, stir, and partially cover the pot until water returns to a boil. Immediately remove cover, stir again, and cook pasta just until al dente. Drain water from pasta, leaving some water clinging to strands, and return to pot, off the heat.

2. Place broiler rack 4 to 5 inches from heat. Preheat broiler.

3. While pasta cooks, heat oil over medium heat in an 8- or 9-inch nonstick skillet. Add garlic and cook for 30 seconds. Add tomatoes and cook uncovered for 3 minutes, stirring occasionally, until tomatoes soften slightly. Transfer to a small bowl. Arrange pasta evenly over bottom of skillet. Spoon tomatoes over pasta.

4. In a large bowl, beat egg substitute, cheese, 1/2 teaspoon salt, and pepper to taste until blended. (If you're using fresh eggs, add 3 tablespoons water to the beaten eggs.) Pour egg mixture into skillet over tomatoes and pasta and cook for about 1 minute. Then lift edges of frittata with a knife, tilting pan slightly so that uncooked egg mixture runs down onto skillet. Repeat as necessary, for 3 to 4 minutes. Transfer to preheated broiler, but make sure handle of skillet sticks out away from the heat. When frittata is set, after about 2 minutes, use a potholder to remove skillet. Lift edges of frittata with a knife to loosen frittata from skillet. Invert frittata onto a serving plate. Sprinkle basil evenly over the top. Cut in half and serve immediately.

2 OUNCES ANGEL HAIR PASTA

2 TEASPOONS OLIVE OIL

1 GARLIC CLOVE, MINCED OR PRESSED

3 RIPE PLUM TOMATOES, CHOPPED INTO 1-INCH CUBES

1 CUP NO-FAT EGG SUBSTITUTE, OR 3 LARGE EGGS

2 TABLESPOONS FRESHLY GRATED PARMESAN CHEESE

1/2 TEASPOON SALT

FRESHLY GROUND BLACK PEPPER, TO TASTE

3 TABLESPOONS CHOPPED FRESH BASIL

SERVES 2

Creamy Lemon Orzo Pudding

This pudding recipe presents a serious rival to rice!

4 CUPS LOW-FAT MILK
1/2 CUP ORZO
1/4 CUP SUGAR
1 LARGE EGG
1 TEASPOON GRATED LEMON PEEL
1/2 TEASPOON VANILLA EXTRACT
1/8 TEASPOON SALT
FRESH MINT SPRIGS AND LEMON PEEL
 TO GARNISH

SERVES 4

1. Heat milk, orzo, and sugar in a medium saucepan over medium-high heat, stirring occasionally, until boiling. Reduce heat to medium low and simmer, stirring occasionally, for 20 minutes, until orzo is tender and mixture thickens.

2. While pasta cooks, beat egg, lemon peel, vanilla, and salt in a medium serving bowl. Add hot orzo mixture, a few tablespoons at a time, stirring constantly, so that egg doesn't curdle. When egg mixture is warm, add orzo mixture in a steady stream, stirring constantly.

3. Cool at room temperature until thickened, about 15 minutes. Garnish with mint and lemon peel. Serve warm or at room temperature.

Peel Ease

The next time you need citrus peel, try this easy method.

Place a strip of plastic wrap over the grater holes to act as a barrier, and to prevent the peel from getting caught between the holes.

Press the lemon firmly into the plastic as you grate to allow the holes' sharp edges to break through the plastic. The peel will appear as soon as this happens.

Pull the plastic gently off the grater when you're done. Using the dull edge of a small knife, scrape the peel from the plastic. Repeat if necessary, using the same strip of plastic.

Mom's Noodle Pudding

The next time you serve roast chicken, surprise your family with this sweet noodle pudding. It's always a treat, either as dessert or as a side dish.

1. Spray an 8-inch square baking pan with nonstick cooking spray or grease lightly. Set aside.

2. In a small bowl, combine bran flake crumbs, brown sugar, and cinnamon. Stir with a fork to mix. Add melted butter and stir until thoroughly combined.

3. Bring 4 quarts of water to a boil in a large covered pot. Add 2 teaspoons salt, if you like. Add pasta, stir, and partially cover the pot until water returns to a boil. Immediately remove cover, stir again, and cook pasta just until al dente. Drain water from pasta and transfer to prepared pan.

4. Preheat the oven to 350° F. While pasta cooks, put the mandarin orange segments with their juices into a food processor or blender. Add cheese, sugar, and egg whites. In a small bowl, mix the cornstarch with 1 tablespoon water until smooth. Add cornstarch paste to the orange mixture and pulse just until oranges are chopped into small pieces. Stir the mixture into the cooked noodles. Crumble Crisp Topping over the pudding.

4. Bake pudding in the preheated oven for 30 to 35 minutes, or until a knife inserted in the center comes out clean. Cool slightly before cutting into squares or rectangles. Serve warm or at room temperature.

CRISP TOPPING

3/4 CUP BRAN FLAKE CEREAL, CRUSHED

1/4 CUP FIRMLY PACKED BROWN SUGAR

1 TEASPOON GROUND CINNAMON

2 TABLESPOONS BUTTER, MELTED

PUDDING

6 OUNCES WIDE NOODLES

1 CAN (11 OUNCES) MANDARIN ORANGE SEGMENTS, UNDRAINED

1/2 CUP PART-SKIM RICOTTA CHEESE OR LOW-FAT COTTAGE CHEESE

3 TABLESPOONS GRANULATED SUGAR

2 LARGE EGG WHITES, LIGHTLY BEATEN

1 TEASPOON CORNSTARCH

SERVES 8

INDEX